Essays in Economics

ELY DEVONS

Essays in Economics

LONDON
GEORGE ALLEN & UNWIN LTD
Ruskin House · Museum Street

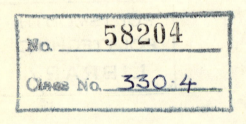
PRINTED IN GREAT BRITAIN
in 11 pt. Bell type
BY SIMSON SHAND LTD
LONDON, HERTFORD AND HARLOW

PREFACE

Seven of the essays and addresses collected together in this volume have already appeared in print, and the thanks of the author are due for permission to reprint. Three, 'Applied Economics—the Application of What?', 'Treasury Control', and 'The Language of Economic Statistics', are published here for the first time. The index of wage-rates, which is explained in detail in the last essay, is now published regularly in the *Manchester School* and *The Guardian*.

Most of the essays are addressed not only to professional economists and economic statisticians, but also to the wider public interested in the uses of economics and economic statistics in public affairs.

E. D.

CONTENTS

PART I

Economics

1

Applied Economics—
The Application of What?[1]

ALTHOUGH I have been an 'applied economist' for many years and have frequently tried to be introspective about my activities, I am, I fear, not yet able to give a clear and methodical account of what it is I am applying. My readers will have to be satisfied, therefore, with random, not very clearly formulated thoughts, almost personal confessions, rather than a carefully worked out systematic treatment.

The main questions I would like to answer are, 'what is it one applies in applied economics?'; 'what is the nature of the understanding of reality one gets through this application?'; 'what use, if any, is this understanding in the formulation of policy?', and lastly, 'what are the best ways of teaching this applied economics?' As I have already indicated, I cannot give satisfactory answers to these questions, but I hope that you agree that they are interesting and important questions.

I am going to divide my argument into three sections. In the first I shall discuss the uses of theory, in the second the other kinds of knowledge which are apparently used in analysing and discussing real economic problems, and in the third I shall discuss teaching.

First then theory and its uses. I cannot, of course, pretend to cover the whole corpus of theory and all possible applications. I shall merely attempt to expound and support my general thesis by illustration and example, although I hope that some of these examples are concerned with the most relevant and important parts of theory. Perhaps it will be as well if I state my general thesis at the outset. This is, that in so far as economic theory is useful in enabling us to understand the real world and in helping us to take decisions on policy, it is the simple, most elementary and, in some ways,

[1] A paper read at the Annual Conference of the Association of Teachers of Economics, December 1958.

most obvious propositions that matter. I do not want, at this stage, to argue whether this is merely a reflection of the present state of economic theory, or whether it is necessarily true of economic theory as such, although this may come up in discussion. I must also emphasize that what I am putting forward is very much a personal view of what theory conveys to me, and you may well think it egotistical arrogance on my part to suggest that such a view is in any way representative.

In putting forward my argument about theory, I want to make a distinction between theoretical models, commonsense axioms, and theoretical concepts.

Two of the most important sets of theoretical models are those of a price system and those of the relation between income, production, employment and expenditure. In both of these it is the elementary propositions conveyed by the models that I find relevant and usable.

Let me take models of the price system first. These are of two kinds. The general, which portray the economy as a whole, and the partial, relating to a single market or to closely interrelated markets. The general models, even of the most elaborate kind, serve the simple purpose of demonstrating the interconnectedness of all economic phenomena, and show how, under certain conditions, price may act as a guiding link between them. Looked at in another way such models show how a complex set of interrelations can hang together consistently without any central administrative direction. They show prices, and the reaction of supply and demand to prices, as the great instruments of co-ordination between dispersed and decentralized decisions. Such models, therefore, give us an understanding of the general principles of operation of the economic system.

These general models are also frequently used as a picture of the perfect economic system, and therefore as providing criteria by which to decide how the real world ought to be made to behave. Such uses of the models are, however, full of pitfalls. For the models are usually static, and the criteria of efficiency and perfection used are themselves highly abstract and axiomatic. Even if the models can be accepted as relevant, it is dangerous to assume that the real world can be made to conform more closely to the model by policy manoeuvres. Real life has other, often more important, aspects apart from the economic, and Government action, which is usually what is prescribed, has many side effects of major importance.

In my view when we get to such problems of applied economics as distribution of industry or monopoly policy, theoretical models of the price system help us little. It is true that argument often proceeds from comparisons between reality and models of perfection. Reality is then easily shown as imperfect, but it is too readily and glibly assumed that an alternative arrangement which it is proposed to put into operation will work perfectly. The real issue of a comparison between the known imperfections of present arrangements and the imperfections of potential alternatives, is one rarely made, and is one in which economic theory can be of little assistance. It is hardly surprising that in such fields of policy there are widely divergent views among economists.

It is in the second, the partial, Marshallian analysis, that I find price theory most useful. The laws of supply and demand, showing price as the mechanism for balancing supply and demand in particular markets, have extensive applications. And is it in their simplest form that they are most useful. Nothing in the way of complicated theory is involved. Let me take two examples to illustrate my view. First, Government or other intervention to fix prices in times of shortage during war or peace. With the simple model of market price as the mechanism for balancing supply and demand, it seems obvious to me as an economist, that if the Government decides to fix a price below that warranted by demand, then some demand which would be prepared to pay a higher price must go unsatisfied. Some arrangement must, therefore, emerge in practice for deciding which demand will go unsatisfied. If these arrangements are left, so to speak to 'natural forces', the situation will be resolved by queues, under the counter dealing, allocation on the basis of friendship or influence, or by breaking the price regulation through a 'black market'. Hence the conclusion that if we do not like such arrangements, the system of price fixing must be accompanied by some enforceable system of rationing. I say enforceable, for unless the Government or other controlling authority can make sure that all supplies will be directed towards the ration, the price control will continue to be frustrated, to a greater or lesser degree, by a black market. From this elementary principle of the 'law of supply and demand', therefore, arises the whole complex of administrative measures that must be taken, and the conditions that must be satisfied, if for some reason it is thought desirable to fix prices below the 'market' level. Similarly, one can consider the relation with supply, and see the effect on supply of any intervention to fix the price above or below that which would result from the market clearing-principle of price.

My second example I take from University salaries. As you know, in the post-war period the Treasury and the UGC, reinforced by pressure from the AUT, and the spirit of the age, have insisted on uniform salaries for the same grades of staff in all subjects. An Assistant Lecturer, whether in History, English, Classics, Physics, or Economic Statistics, must be paid the same salary. When I, as an economist, consider this insistence on uniformity, I see it in relation to the relative conditions of supply and demand of staff in these different subjects. And I come to the conclusion that if these conditions are different for different subjects, then the formal insistence on uniformity will have some peculiar consequences. The exact consequences I cannot tell in advance, but the kind of thing I expect might happen, and am not surprised by, is along the following lines. Suppose the salary is fixed at a level which merely calls forth an adequate supply in the popular Arts subjects, then it is unlikely to call forth an adequate supply in such subjects as Engineering, Physics, Accounting or Economic Statistics. Since Assistant Lecturers will be difficult to obtain in these subjects, the Departments concerned will try, if the University system will let them, to appoint at the Lecturer level instead. If they get permission to do this, the net result will be that they will appoint as Lecturers staff of an age and with post-graduate experience comparable with Assistant Lecturers in such subjects as Languages and History where supply is more plentiful. Alternatively, if the general level of Assistant Lecturer salaries is such as to attract an adequate supply in the 'scarce' subjects, then in the 'Arts' subjects the supply will be superabundant, and the best candidates getting the Assistant Lecturer posts may have ten years or more research experience after graduation.

The point I am trying to make in these examples—and

many others of a similar kind could, of course be given—is that the economic theory used in analysing the situation for policy purposes is of the most elementary kind, very little beyond what is contained in the first chapters of Henderson's 'Supply and Demand'. But do not mistake my point, for I am not arguing that the understanding or results obtained from the application of the theory are themselves trivial. On the contrary, I think they are most valuable and important, and ignorance of them can lead to confusion and chaos in policy making. Nor does it follow from the simplicity of the propositions that they are easy to teach others to absorb into their way of thinking. Again, it is characteristic of the situation, that while an economist would approach the two sets of problems in the way I have explained, this approach would not normally occur to the administrator in the Civil Service or to the politician, or to non-economists in the University world. And even though some of them, and I emphasize *some*, might appreciate the point when put to them, they are unlikely to absorb it in such a way as to apply the principle, simple though it may be, to new situations.

The second group of models I want to refer to, to support my argument, are those which are used in discussion and decision about policy affecting the general level of economic activity. Here again I feel that however elaborate the theoretical models, econometric and other, it is the most simple and elementary elements in them which are used and are usable. Little more theory to my mind is used in policy making than the notion that income, production, employment and expenditure are all closely interrelated, and that in maintaining employment and production it is 'effective demand' that matters. That if there are forces in operation making for a decline in production and employment, the way to restore them is by increasing effective demand, and vice versa.

We have perhaps got a little beyond this in dividing expenditure into what we regard as significant categories, and we use these divisions both in an attempt to analyse the determinants of fluctuations in expenditure, and in deciding how to influence these. We look separately at Government expenditure, construction, plant and equipment, stocks, consumption and exports. But we have little usable knowledge in terms of general propositions about what determines

B

fluctuations in expenditure in each of these divisions. All that theory seems to tell me at present is that I ought to watch each of these separately, since they are subject to different influences, and changes in them have differing consequences. A good deal of the argument about economic policy results from differing views about what is happening or likely to happen to any one or all of these, and in relation to any particular diagnosis, from differences of view about the relative effectiveness and social and political desirability of particular policies for influencing them.

I know that there are also great controversies about the clash between domestic and foreign trade policies, about the risks that should be run in having unemployment, about the advantages or disadvantages of a rising price level, and the effect of these on the level of economic activity and the rate of economic progress. But to me the present contribution that theory makes to the analysis of these problems is not far short of trivial. Arguments between economists advocating one policy rather than another, can usually be explained more significantly in terms of politics rather than economics. They develop into unedifying slanging matches, in which each faction picks out those particular elements or that particular formulation of the problem which lead to the conclusion it favours.

I now turn to a rather different group of notions which we get from theory, but which do not imply theoretical propositions in the same way as those which I have just been discussing. For want of a better term, I call these common sense maxims about the economic facts of life. Some of them are axioms of logical behaviour, others are general truths to keep in mind in trying to understand what goes on in the real world. Some in the first category are 'bygones are bygones', 'you cannot have your cake and eat it', 'in full employment, other things being equal, using more resources one way means using less in others', 'real costs are opportunity costs'. In the second category are such general truths as 'all transactions are two-sided, for every purchase there must be a sale', 'the balance of payments must balance', or slightly more subtle ones, 'changes in stocks are merely another way of expressing the relation between output and consumption', and the one made famous by Marshall, 'Natura non facit saltum'.

I have always found that propositions of this kind play an important role in understanding what goes on in economic life and in arguments about economic policy. Take one or two examples. The notion that with resources fully employed you cannot have more of anything without giving up something else, played an extremely important part in all war-time economic planning. Arguing about the choice of one thing rather than another, explaining the cost of the choice in terms of other potential uses of the resources involved, ensuring the consistency of different choices, was in all its various aspects the day to day activity of many economists temporarily employed in the Civil Service in war-time. In this activity they were using little more than the simple maxims of consistent logical behaviour, arguing that two and two make four and never five. True the working out of this logic in practice was most complex, for it involved taking account of time, for example in considering the relation between the build up of munitions factories, munitions output and the size of the armed forces, and it implied a knowledge of facts, for example, about the ease with which resources could be moved from one use to another; but the general principles or maxims being used were of the most elementary kind.

Or take the maxim that 'bygones are bygones'. It was because economists used this notion that there was so frequently a difference between them and the accountants, civil servants, and business men about the advisability of Government encouragement for extensive investment in the cotton industry after the war. In considering the worthwhileness of investment in automatic looms for instance, the accountants usually insisted on the comparison being made on the basis of newly purchased automatic and non-automatic looms. The economists on the other hand argued that there were plenty of non-automatic looms already in existence, long since written off, but usable for many years ahead, and that the estimates of capital costs on non-automatic looms should, therefore, be taken very near zero.

Of the general truths which are important to keep in mind in trying to understand what goes on in the real world, I would pick out for special mention 'the double nature of economic transactions' and 'natura non facit saltum'. The importance of these can be judged from the error into which people are led by ignoring them. How frequently do people discuss the potential threat to the rest of the world of increased exports from the European Common Market without paying attention to the implication that this would mean increased imports into Europe too? Or refer to the opportunities open to some British industries for expanding exports in the European Free Trade Area—when this was still a possibility—without realizing that this would mean increased imports into this country. How frequently do students talk about sales of gilt-edged, and appear rather non-plussed when asked who buys them from the sellers? Or do you remember the immediate post-war period, when the use of the word 'inflation' was still taboo, and Government propaganda—from the Ministry of Labour particularly—kept on plugging the idea that we were suffering from 'an overall man-power shortage'. If we could only increase the labour force all would be well! In the way the argument was presented to the public, the fact that this would also mean increased incomes, was completely overlooked. All simple errors, but how easy to fall into them, and how disastrous the consequences if policy is based on misapprehensions of this kind.

The Marshallian maxim that 'natura non facit saltum' is ignored in the 'all or nothing' view which the public usually takes of economic affairs. Such slogans as 'Export or Die', or popular assessment at the time of the Suez crisis of the economic importance of the Suez Canal, are based on a complete misunderstanding of the nature of economic activity. The public seemed to be under the impression that the closing of the Suez Canal would bring British industry to a standstill. In fact adjustments at the margin in fuel supplies and consumption, and in the use of alternative shipping routes, together with the availability of stocks, meant that the affect was quite small. It is indeed now very difficult to pick out the 'Suez crisis' period in the figures of production and trade. Here again the way in which economists look at these issues, in emphasizing that the possibilities of substitution at the margin are many and varied, and that issues of policy are really about marginal changes, is of great value in correcting public misunderstanding.

Lastly, in this section on theory, I turn to theoretical concepts which I think of as a special short-hand language which economists have invented for describing economic relations. Many of these play an important part in the theoretical models which I discussed earlier, but I am not here thinking of them in that context but as parts of an economic language unrelated to any particular theory. Such terms as elasticity, mobility, competition, substitution, short-period, long-period, net advantages, equilibrium, marginal and so on. These are used in applied economics and discussions of policy mainly as a short-hand language. And in my view they normally contribute no more than this. They do, of course, make it possible for economists to talk to each other in a jargon of their own, which excludes outsiders from the conversation, and in some circumstances this gives the profession a certain prestige. This is perhaps in itself a fairly harmless form of vanity, but the position is more pathetic when economists by using the language merely deceive themselves. For the use of the language may give the illusion of great understanding, whereas in fact it often merely conceals ignorance in a mass of esoteric jargon. And it is so easy and dangerous to mistake description and classification of situations in a special economic language as answers to problems.

So much for theory. I now turn to the other kinds of knowledge used in applied economics. These are mainly factual, and are of two kinds, statistical and institutional. The information about institutions may be merely descriptive or may also attempt to give some understanding of how the institutions work. I have less to say about the application of this kind of knowledge than about theory, for I find it even more difficult with this to distinguish between the illusion of understanding and real understanding.

Take statistical information first. There is, of course, a passion for statistical information in relation to any and every issue of economic policy. Indeed the normal first reaction of any economist today considering a real problem for the first time is to complain of the inadequacy of the statistics available. And yet how often do we really honestly ask ourselves what we get out of the figures? True they give us a comforting feeling that we know a great deal, and they enable us to take ourselves or others on an impressive statistical tour of some part of the economy—what we usually call, 'an appreciation of the situation'. Once this kind of activity reaches a certain level, it grows and spreads by its own power. For Government Departments, business, and organs of publicity and education, feel the need to have economists who can write appreciations for them and argue about and interpret those made by others. But where essentially does it get us? Are we any better off than the commentators on politics and foreign affairs who can give us exquisitely neat and tidy analyses of the current political and international scene, but can tell us precious little about what we should expect to happen next, or what is the best way of dealing with the situation?

Take the analysis of the present economic situation. We can write a detailed statistical appreciation quite readily, drawing attention to all the important elements in the situation. This is no doubt of value in telling us where we are, but it gives us precious little clue to what is going to happen next. I do not want to decry the importance of the knowledge that we get from statistical appreciations of this kind, but merely to suggest that we should be careful not to kid ourselves, let alone others, that from the mere accumulation of such appreciations comes greater understanding.

At least, however, appreciations of the general economic situation are directed to helping Government or business in decisions which they have to take. What about statistical appreciations which have no obvious pointed direction of this kind? I well remember asking myself this question after giving a lecture a few years ago, called 'The Economist looks at the Coal Industry', to a Conference of Colliery Managers. I had warned the man who asked me to do this that I knew nothing about the coal industry, and he said 'fine, just what we want. A fresh mind, with no preconceived prejudices'. In the end I succumbed and gave what I suppose is a fairly typical paper in applied economics. Apart from deploying the usual arguments for changing pricing policy for coal— arguments which used the elementary theoretical notions I discussed earlier—my main themes were statistical, although these were filled out with quite a lot of patter. Some of the themes I dealt with were: the importance of coal in the

economy as a whole, the effect on the balance of payments of
the loss of coal exports, the main trends in coal consumption,
fuel costs as a proportion of total costs in industry, the importance of fuel in consumers' expenditure, movements in
coal prices compared with other prices, and so on. I do not
believe I am being arrogant when I say that the lecture went
down well, and there were many comments afterwards on
how enlightening my talk had been. And yet as I drove back
to Manchester I found it difficult to answer the question—in
what way enlightening? I had put to my audience a number of
facts about the coal industry of which they were obviously
previously ignorant, and no doubt this enabled them to see
the problems of the coal industry in a broader perspective. I
had also attempted to correct some mistaken popular notions, for example about the rise in coal prices compared with
other prices since before the war. But was there anything
beyond this?

Indeed a good deal of the use of economic statistics by the
applied economist in public discussion seems to be of this
negative kind—correcting mistaken notions of facts which
have for some mysterious reason bitten deep into the public
mind. When politicians and others go around arguing that we
are in trouble because we do not pay our way overseas, one
can quote the balance of payments figures of the last ten
years. One can attempt to correct mistaken popular notions
about relative rates of economic progress in the US and UK
since the war, by quoting some of the statistical evidence. In
the Suez situation which I have referred to earlier, it would
have been very valuable if one could have got across to the
public some of the statistics about the fuel and shipping
situation. And as no doubt misconceptions of fact will continue in the future as in the past, the economist who is
sufficiently interested and familiar with the statistics, will
continue to find a useful application for his knowledge in
telling others what nonsense they are talking.

Economic statistics sometimes play a role in economic
policy which is different from that which I have been discussing, and although not directly related to my central theme,
it may nevertheless be worth mentioning. I have in mind
those statistics which assume great importance in the public
mind and may influence the public a great deal in the action

they themselves take or the action they demand from the Government. Take two sets of statistics of this kind which have significance, the figures of gold and foreign exchange reserves and the unemployment percentage. The evidence before the Bank Rate Tribunal showed what an important influence figures of the reserves had on the views of people in the City of London about the underlying trading position of this country, and therefore on their actions and decisions. Indeed one is sometimes tempted to take the view that there might be fewer speculative balance of payments crises if the gold and foreign exchange reserve figures were not published. Again the unemployment percentage appears to have a most powerful influence in politics. Great significance is apparently attached to whether or not it is below the magical 3 per cent. The fact that the figure is quite differently calculated and has quite a different significance from before 1948 and pre-war, is completely overlooked. Indeed the public reaction to statistics of this kind is something which any astute economic politician is bound to take into account. But I doubt whether he would get much help on this from the applied economist. Here is a field for the economic psychologist or sociologist.

The other kind of factual knowledge is mainly about institutions. A good deal of applied economics, in banking, finance, industrial relations and industrial organization is descriptive of institutions and how they work. Let me take the organization of industry as an example, for I am more familiar with this than with the others. In what is written about industrial organization, there is usually a little potted history and technology, some statistics about the size of firms, production and outlets, and then usually some attempt to discuss whether the industry is efficient or not. This may involve some attempt to analyse the extent of competition, restrictive practices, and the use of monopoly power. This is, for example, a fairly standard pattern in that extensive, but much delayed, symposium, edited by Duncan Burn, on the Structure of British Industry.

Here again my reaction is that the nature and usefulness of the understanding one gets is of a most elusive kind. Usually, if the job is well done, one gets the impression, I think quite rightly, that economic organizations are most complex in their variety and ways of working, that it is dangerous to think in terms of simple generalizations, and that sweeping proposals for reforming an industry or organization are dangerously deceptive. If this view is correct it means, again, that the usefulness of this kind of understanding is largely of a negative kind. For it merely enables one to talk with some apparent authority to people who are obviously ignorant about the affairs of the industry, and to comment on and criticize proposals for public intervention of one kind or another.

The one thing which is usually missing from such analysis and understanding is any reference to problems of internal organization, administration and decision taking, and therefore any clue to what makes some firms and institutions efficient and successful and others inefficient and failures. Certainly this is true of my own contribution on the 'Aircraft Industry' to the Burn symposium. I spent quite a lot of time on this and can now pose, compared with those who know nothing, as something of an 'expert' on the economics of the industry. But on such important questions as 'what has made Rolls-Royce such an efficient and successful firm?', I am as perplexed as ever.

I now come to my third section. How does one teach applied economics? This is the most difficult question of all and the difficulty for me at least is partly due to the fact that I have not been successful in answering clearly and precisely the prior questions about what it is we are applying.

If you agree with my general argument that what we are applying in theory are the elementary propositions and commonsense maxims, it might seem to follow that it should be fairly easy to teach students of economics to discuss real economic issues critically and intelligently. But this is not so, in my experience at least. Students seem to be able to master theory as theory and even to deal with notional applications of theory, but when it comes to discussing some real problem on which they have not been specifically instructed, they seem to be influenced more by notions they derive from TV or the popular daily Press than anything they have learnt in Economics.

Clearly one of the most difficult things to achieve is to get the student in a position in which the elementary propositions and maxims are part of his normal processes of thinking, and are not kept in a separate compartment labelled 'economic theory'. One way of doing this is to take him through examples of the theory in as many different contexts as possible. The laws of supply and demand in relation to commodities, factors of production, location of industry, international trade, etc. It also seems to be true that the elementary propositions will not be absorbed if the theoretical instruction is merely kept to the elementary level. It is only when the student has been through a theoretical drill well beyond the elementary level that the elementary notions really sink in deep.

But it is, of course, not enough to learn the theory as theory. In some way the bridge to application to real economic situations must be crossed. It is here I think that at present we make the biggest mistakes. First because there is a tendency to show how the theory can be applied to get solutions, whereas, to my mind at least, we ought to concentrate on showing how the theory illumines the nature of the problems. Secondly because it is the big issues, the control of inflation, devaluation, agricultural policy, nationalization, that are given to him as the important issues of application. He is expected, judging by examination papers, to provide solutions to the most difficult current economic problems. At the end of three years, if not earlier, the student is encouraged to see himself as an exceptional Chancellor of the Exchequer, who could put everything right if he were only given half a chance.

I think this is disastrous, and that we must in some way try to teach him applications of a less ambitious kind. The trouble is that these are not very easy to find, for most of the literature is about the great issues of public policy. But the two examples I gave earlier of the operation of the elementary propositions in supply and demand theory are the kind of examples I have in mind.

The other thing we should do is to make the student suspicious of slogans in economic policy, and to make him understand why he should be suspicious. But it is my impression that far from doing this many teachers of economics, in fact, feed their students with slogans: 'Invest more', 'Increase the Gold and Foreign Exchange Reserves', 'Double the standard of living in 25 years'. I do not want to argue whether or not these are good slogans for policy makers. My main point is that this is not the way to turn the young student into an applied economist, capable of thinking for himself.

The other puzzling question is how to get across to the student some of the knowledge both statistical and institutional, that I talked about in my second section. I have tried to get students to learn to read economic statistics, and to write statistical appreciations about some aspect of the working of the economic system, but I have not been very successful. I am forced to the conclusion that this aspect of understanding, for what it is worth, is acquired only by long painful apprenticeship, and with some, as is only too patently obvious, it is never acquired at all.

In trying to convey an understanding of how institutions work, one is perpetually up against the difficulty of discussing problems of economic administration with students who have never had experience of an administrative problem in their lives. And to those without such experience such problems are usually either completely baffling, or obviously the result of stupid inefficiency. If the student can be induced to get a job in a firm or Government Department for a few weeks, not to earn a lot of money, but to see something of the working of an institution in practice, it is much easier to discuss such problems with him afterwards.

Before I conclude I feel I must apologise for not having answered more adequately the questions I posed at the beginning of this paper, although I hope I have given you something to argue about. I do really feel that in thirteen pages of rather discursive argument I have got little beyond what Keynes stated so succinctly in the first two sentences of his introduction to the Cambridge Economic Handbooks nearly forty years ago—'The Theory of Economics does not furnish a body of settled conclusions immediately applicable to policy. It is a method rather than a doctrine, an apparatus of mind, a technique of thinking, which helps its possessor to draw correct conclusions.'

POSTSCRIPT

In pondering over the discussion of my paper at Southampton, I think the following points worth noting. These are not meant as a summary of the discussion, but merely some of the points I would try to cover if I were rewriting the paper.

1. My paper was not meant to be 'an attack on theory'. I was merely trying to answer the question 'what part of *present* theory is enlightening and usable?' If anything my remarks about the use of economic statistics and descriptive economics were more damning than my comments on theory. For I argued that there are useful elements in theory, but that I saw little point, except of a negative kind, either for understanding or for policy, in most statistical and empirical descriptions of the economy.

2. By what criteria does one decide whether theoretical propositions are 'elementary and simple'?

Is it true that theory which is complex and difficult to use for the initiating generation, is simple and useful for the next generation (e.g. by analogy with physics, theories taught today to schoolboys of sixteen were complex and difficult even for eminent physicists thirty years ago)? That theory which is apparently complicated and unusable today, will appear simple and useful to economists in thirty years' time? If this is so, then my argument that only elementary and simple theory is useful, would, to some extent at least, be tautalogical.

I do not think that this is so. It is not that theory becomes useful as time passes, because the theory, originally thought complex, progressively appears simpler as it is absorbed into general thinking. My argument is that, whether or not this happens, it is the simpler aspects of the theory which are usable. I admit that it is difficult to disentangle complexity and simplicity from strangeness and familiarity. But in price and value theory, for example, although much of what was strange and difficult twenty-five years ago is familiar and easy today (i.e. what was advanced economic theory then now appears in first year courses), it is still the simple and elementary aspect of what continues to be a complex theory which is usable. (Price theory would appear strange and complex to an African brought up in a primitive economy with a traditional exchange system, but when he had got over the strangeness it would still only be the elementary aspects of the theory, i.e. the general laws of supply and demand, that he would find useful.)

3. What do I mean by 'theory'? This is obviously not easy to answer. Certainly not just any general idea or proposition with which one approaches the study of reality. In this sense, theory is always involved, if merely by implication. Even in an apparently theory-free description of the facts, some general propositions are implied in deciding which facts are worth including in the description.

By theory I had in mind the formulation of a model in which the relation between the elements being considered was expressed, or could be expressed, mathematically. This is what to my mind 'economic theory' has essentially been in the past, and continues to be today.

In attempting to understand reality, one can use models of this kind. The models may or may not be formulated in such a way that they are in principle testable. Even when in principle they are testable, there remain the complications, statistical and other, in relating them to complex reality.

The alternative approach to understanding is what in the discussion at Southampton I called 'the historian's technique'. I do not mean by this trying to find 'laws of trends in history', but the approach to reality which tried to understand what is going on by 'soaking oneself in the facts of the situation'. In this approach one has no precise model clearly formulated in advance which one is testing against reality. One may, however, have certain general considerations in mind of what are important elements in the situation, and one approaches the facts within this kind of vague framework.

4. Is further progress in economic understanding, which will be usable for policy, more likely to be made by the 'theorist's' or the 'historian's' technique? There is clearly not a priori logical basis on which one can argue that one will always be more fruitful than the other. The proof of the pudding must be in the eating. But there are certain characteristics of the two which are of some importance:

(a) The theoretical approach usually implies the specification in advance of the model which is to be tested. The danger here is that in the testing process facts that do not fit into the framework of the model will be ignored. It is difficult both to specify logically the model in advance and to be flexible in using it in studying reality. The ideal of 'a closed model and an open mind' is difficult to achieve.

In any case a theoretical model cannot be based on mere introspection and thought about logical relations. It must have some relation to reality, and the appropriate elements of reality to assume can only be selected by some process other than that of model building.

It does not seem to be possible at present sensibly to formulate some of the problems in which we are interested in the form of theoretical models of this kind. If, therefore, we insist on this method as *the correct* way of conducting research, we either produce rather silly models or say that we cannot deal with these problems.

(b) The 'historian's technique' is open to the danger that since we do not clearly specify in advance what we are looking for, we run the danger of merely collecting facts for facts sake, and may end up without learning anything very useful. Even where we have some general propositions vaguely in mind, the element of personal judgment in assessing the facts in relation to these propositions may be very large, and therefore two people approaching the same facts may come to quite different conclusions. This indeed very frequently happens among historians, each historian giving his own interpretation.

5. There are many problems which to my mind cannot be sensibly investigated at present with the theoretical approach. Take two which were discussed at Southampton:

(a) First the relative importance of 'security' and 'competition' as elements in economic progress. No doubt some ingenious theorist could formulate a model which included these as dynamic variables and could produce a solution giving the optimum situation. But I find it difficult to envisage such a model being useful either as a research tool or for policy.

If one wants to investigate this problem one must, at present at least, proceed by the historian's method.

That is, try to examine, in relation to a particular industry or group of industries, what the relation between the factors appears to be. In doing this one might try to proceed by the comparative method, but this would involve much judgment. For it is unlikely that one would find a series of pairs of industries apparently similar in all respects, except that the firms in one experienced great uncertainty about the future because of fierce competition, and in the other enjoyed great security because of monopolistic structure or restrictive agreements. One must be prepared to conclude that in some situations 'security' and in others 'competition' appears more conducive to progress, without being able to specify in general terms what the differences in the two sets of situations are.[1] The results for policy making would then be, as they frequently are, that 'each situation must be judged on its merits'. Such a conclusion would not be very helpful, but I cannot envisage that proceeding by trying to test more formal models would at present get us any further. This does not mean, however, that those who think they can get further by this route should be discouraged from trying.

(b) Second, one problem I mentioned in my paper, 'What makes Rolls-Royce an efficient aero-engine firm?' Here to my mind we do not have any of the elements for formulating even a tentative model in advance. One may have vague ideas, e.g. that it has all depended on the personality of Lord Hives (the great man theory of business efficiency?), but these are so uncertain that, even in principle, I do not see how one could specify in advance what general propositions one was going to try to test. My view would be that if one was attempting to answer a question of this kind, one would have to go and work inside Rolls-Royce for some time, starting with an open (almost blank!) mind, only formulating views as one progressively soaked in more and more evidence about what made the firm tick.

[1] Indeed one must also be prepared to emerge with a conclusion that neither factor, competition nor security, had much bearing on economic progress.

6. Given the views expressed in (4) and (5), there cannot to my mind be any logical guiding principles on which to allocate resources between different methods of research. This must inevitably be a matter for personal interest, capacity and judgment (sometimes called prejudice).

2

The Role of the Economist
in Public Affairs[1]

I

THE public's attitude to the economist is full of contradictions. Sometimes he is treated as an expert who understands the workings of our highly complex economic system, and whose voice and advice must, therefore, be listened to. On other occasions he is dismissed as theoretical, unrealistic, narrow and hard-hearted. The profession of economists as a whole is frequently accused of adding confusion rather than clarification to public debate, by disagreeing so violently among themselves, and offering conflicting advice on crucial issues: 'Where there are two economists', it is said, 'there will be three opinions'.

This situation is partly the fault of economists, partly that of the public. Economists speak and write in a jargon which, while it may make it easier for them to communicate with one another, impedes communication with the public. And the jargon may often be used more to impress the public with the esoteric nature of the economist's knowledge than to facilitate public appreciation of the true nature of the economist's understanding.

The extent of this understanding may be limited, but the solution of crises and difficult issues will not await on the improvement of that understanding. Policies have to be decided to deal with these issues and the public expect and demand answers from the economists. Modern society wishes to exercise control over its economic destiny and demands that economists should give it the means to exercise that control. It is hardly surprising, therefore, that economists sometimes cannot resist the flattery and prestige that acceptance of this role implies; nor that the public, having elevated the economist to this central position, should every now and again

[1] *Lloyds Bank Review*, July 1959.

C

become dissatisfied and disillusioned, when events prove that the economist is incapable of providing what the public demands.

Issues of economic policy are necessarily issues of politics. Even in theory it is difficult to distinguish between the economic and political aspects of a problem. Once the problem gets into the public arena, economics and politics are inevitably inextricably interwoven—and when the economist engages in public debate he is necessarily involved in politics. It is here that one of the main sources of difficulty arises. For, even if the economist tries to distinguish between the economic and political elements in his argument, the public is unlikely to recognize the distinction. To the public an economist is an economist, and most people are not usually able, even if they were willing, to distinguish the political from the economic. Nor does the economist always try to help. Since economics has a certain prestige as being scientific, the economist is likely to succumb to the temptation, consciously or otherwise, of arguing in support of a particular policy on economic grounds, without revealing the political implications or assumptions in his argument.

There is no easy way out of these difficulties. But we might go some way towards dealing with them if there were a greater willingness on the part of economists to explain to the public the limits to the usefulness of their understanding in contributing to policy decisions, and a greater willingness on the part of the public not to demand or expect too much from the economist. It would be foolish and presumptuous to suggest that in a short article one can fully explore the whole field of economics and economic policy to see the essential nature of the contribution the economist makes, and to hope to explain and dispel the sources of confusion and misunderstanding. All that I can attempt is to give some indication of the way in which I see these issues. It is characteristic of the situation I have already referred to that no doubt many of my fellow economists will disagree violently with the views I put forward.

II

The knowledge that the economist uses in analysing economic problems and in giving advice on them is of three kinds.

First, theories of how the economic system works (and why it sometimes does not work so well); second, commonsense maxims about reasonable economic behaviour; and third, knowledge of the facts describing the main features of the economy, many of these facts being statistical. I take these in turn and comment on the contribution such knowledge can make in leading to sensible decisions on public issues.

Modern economic theory in many of its branches is highly complex and often mathematical. There is frequent controversy among economists themselves about how much of this theory is merely an intellectual toy, and how much can be expected at some stage to be useful in helping us to understand the working of the economy and to influence its working. Much of this controversy is barren and inconclusive, for one can never tell in advance in any subject which lines of theoretical exploration will eventually yield most fruit. The important point for our purpose is that, whatever may be true in the future, today most of this complex theory is not useful in helping to deal with real economic issues. If it is introduced into the arena of public debate, as it sometimes is, it merely serves to confuse the public, and to conceal the fact that it is the simplest propositions only which have relevance to the issues under consideration.

The general theories which are usable and are used most often are of the simplest kind. Two of the most important are the elementary propositions showing the functional relation between the supply, price and demand for any particular commodity or service (usually referred to as 'the laws of supply and demand'); and those showing the relation between income, expenditure, production and employment for the economy as a whole—Keynesian economics and its statistical counterpart, national income accounting.

The elementary 'laws of supply and demand' have a very wide range of applications. Their significance is frequently ignored by the public and the government, and, by drawing attention to the way in which they might work out in particular situations, the economist can try to ensure that policies are embarked on only with a full knowledge of their implications and consequences. When economists argue that rent control, which means fixing rents below the price that would occur in a free market, leads to a queue for housing, unwillingness to build houses for rent, a tendency for landlords to neglect to repair their property, difficulty in persuading tenants to move, the development of lump-sum key money payments, etc. etc., they are using no more economic theory than the elementary notion that rents are a price relating the supply and the demand for housing. When, as frequently happens in the spring before the new crop is available, the price of old potatoes rises and some sections of the public clamour for the government to intervene to control the price, the economist argues that the rise in price is not the cause but the result of the shortage. In such circumstances if the government intervened to fix the price, since the supply cannot be increased, the limited supplies would be allocated by other means—queueing, black-market dealing, favouritism, influence, etc. Again in arguing in this way the economist is using nothing beyond the most elementary theory. Very much the same is true in discussions about the implications and consequences of agricultural price-fixing and subsidies, international commodity schemes, equal pay for men and women, national uniform rates of pay for particular occupations, taxation of particular commodities or types of incomes. It is indeed remarkable what a wide application these simple 'laws' have.

The fact that they are simple does not, however, mean that they are unimportant, or that they are always kept in mind. On the contrary, they are of the greatest significance and ignoring them may lead to the most wasteful and frustrating mistakes. It is the fact that the economist has absorbed these laws as part of his normal apparatus of thinking that makes his potential contribution so important.

Sometimes 'the laws of supply and demand' are quoted as 'natural' and any intervention to control supply, demand or price, is said to be an offence against 'nature'. This is, of course, nonsense. It may be argued that interference has such consequences that it would be better to leave things to the 'free market'; but to bless the 'free market' as 'natural' and intervention as 'unnatural' merely confuses the issue.

To turn to the second of the general propositions mentioned above, it is true that Keynesian theory and post-Keynesian developments of the theory are, in their academic form, complex and full of niceties and refinements which give rise to continuing argument and controversy. But the essential parts of the theory which are useful at present in general discussion about economic policy are simple and limited; little more than the notion that employment, production, income and expenditure are closely interrelated. If there is full employment and full use of capacity an increase in expenditure will lead to bottlenecks, shortages and price increases; and if there is unemployment and under-utilization of capacity, actual or potential, this can be remedied by increasing expenditure. A similar set of ideas is used in discussing the problems of the balance of payments, and the effects on the balance of changes in expenditure at home. Increasing expenditure at home will divert exports to the home market and draw in imports; decreasing expenditure at home will reduce imports and divert goods to exports. These effects will, however, be influenced by what is happening to expenditure in other countries.

A large part of the regular analysis of the general economic situation in government publications, such as the *Economic Survey*, in the *Economic Review* of the National Institute of Economic and Social Research, and in the London and Cambridge *Economic Bulletin*, is concerned with exploring this relationship, both actual and prospective, between income, production and expenditure, and between home expenditure and foreign trade. These analyses are, to my mind, based essentially on elementary theoretical ideas. The reason they appear complex to the layman is that they are conducted in statistical terms. It is the elaborate technical methods and conventions employed in making the statistical estimates of national income, production and expenditure and the balance of payments which are used in this analysis, rather than any complexity of the theoretical analysis itself, which makes all this such a mystery to the outsider. Even for the economist himself it is quite a task to learn sufficient about the meaning and method of calculation of the figures in the Blue Book on National Income and Expenditure and the White Papers on the Balance of Payments to be able to use them without falling into error! When argument about the economic situation is conducted in this esoteric statistical language, how easy it is for the public to get the impression that this implies intricate and involved theory. And how tempting for the economist to leave them with this illusion, and even to play on it to increase the prestige of the profession!

III

There are many commonsense maxims of economic life which play a great role in debate about public issues, and these again are essentially simple notions. Take for example the maxim that you cannot get more than a pint out of a pint pot, alternatively expressed in economic jargon as 'if resources are fully employed then, barring increases in productivity, the production of more of some things implies less of others'. This was the main idea behind many of the contributions of economists to war-time economic planning: that, other things being equal, calling up more men into the armed forces meant less munitions production or less supplies for civilian use or less of both; or that it was wasteful to call men up if there were not going to be the munitions for them, and so on. Similarly in the period of acute post-war shortages, the argument that more public expenditure on health, education or defence meant less private expenditure on consumption or investment. These examples and others of a similar kind merely draw attention to the logic of choice and the idea of opportunity cost: whether in the household, the firm, or the country as a whole, having more of one thing means giving up something else, other things being equal (i.e. unless you borrow or otherwise increase the total available). If you act as if you can get more of everything at the same time, when in fact total production is limited, you are liable to get into a frustrated, tangled mess.

From this follows the prescription; choose logically and consistently in advance! This prescription, however, often makes the public furious with the economist. For human beings in their collective as well as in their individual lives are often impulsive, illogical and inconsistent, and prefer to be so. The alternative is so-called cold-blooded, inhuman calculation! Indeed Utopias of perfectly rational individuals all choosing logically and consistently by calculation are repulsive even to economists. Is it any wonder that when economists preach consistent and rational calculation, the public should sometimes feel like stoning them?

The logic of choice is, however, sometimes falsely presented, especially in statistical terms. Very often expenditure on some particular item is calculated as a percentage of the national income, and then it is argued that because that percentage is small (or large), or because it is smaller (or larger) than in some previous year, or in some other country, this shows that more (or less) ought to be devoted to that particular item. This is done frequently in argument about domestic or foreign investment, contributions to the development of backward areas, expenditure on health, education, or the roads, etc., I have frequently argued against the use of percentages in this way. At most, comparisons of this kind may give a *prima facie* case for looking in detail at the expenditure concerned and examining carefully the case for spending more or less. The notion that there is a right percentage to spend, and that this can be discovered by looking at past years or other countries, is most misleading.

I have dealt at some length with this simple maxim of logical choice because it is so important, enters almost automatically into an economist's way of thinking, but is quite strange to many other people. But there are many other commonsense truisms of this kind, such as 'the balance of payments must balance', 'bygones are bygones', 'where there is a purchase there is also a sale', none of which involve any abstruse theory but all of which are used frequently by the economist in argument about policy.

IV

Much argument about policy proceeds on mistaken ideas of the facts, and knowledge of the facts enables the economist to contradict error and dispel myths and illusions. The most potent facts in public debate are statistics, since these are thought to represent hard reality. The mass of statistical data about our economic affairs is now so overwhelming that any one economist can only be sufficiently expert in part of them to know what they portray and to be able to use them without error. I dealt in some detail with the use and abuse of statistics in economic policy in another article in this *Review*

in July 1954,[1] and I will not again enlarge on these issues. It
is, however, relevant to my argument here to stress that the
accumulation of statistics about a particular economic problem or about the general economic situation, apart from enabling the economist to point out factual errors in other
people's arguments, may add little to his understanding or
to his capacity to advise on important issues of policy. It
may give him the comfortable feeling that he knows a lot
about some particular corner of the economy, and enable
him to take others on an impressive statistical tour—what
is called 'an appreciation of the situation'. But these appreciations may be of little more use than the exquisitely neat and tidy
analyses of the commentators on politics and foreign affairs.

V

So far I have discussed some of those aspects of the understanding and knowledge that the economist has which seem
at present to be useful in public debate about economic policy.
If public debate and decision were confined to these, all might
be well. But, of course, it cannot be, and is not so confined.
Issues of economic policy do not await on the understanding
of economists. Problems come up, decisions have to be taken
(even if the decision is, by default, one of no action),
whether economists can give clear answers or not. It is here
that the main difficulty and source of confusion and misunderstanding arises.

It is useful to distinguish two different sets of issues. First,
those where, although the economist has something useful to
contribute, what he has to say is not enough for those who
have to decide. The second, where the controversy among
economists on the fundamental forces in operation is such
that there are a whole range of views, some of them completely opposing, on offer to pick from.

Issues of the first kind arise in some applications of the
'laws of supply and demand' or in some uses of the theory of
the relation between 'income, production and expenditure'
which were discussed above. The economist may be able to
say that if the government puts an extra tax on television
sets, then the demand will fall; that if oil prices fall relatively

---

[1] 'Statistics as a Basis for Policy', included as Essay 7 in this collection.

to coal prices, the demand for coal will fall; or that if the government fixes a guaranteed price for milk the supply of milk will be affected. But answering the question 'by how much will the demand for television sets or coal fall?', or 'what will be the supply of milk at a particular price?', is much more difficult. Valiant attempts are being made to give quantitative answers to questions of this kind but progress is slow and uncertain, and the answers have to be used with caution.

But it is one thing to attempt to answer the limited question 'what would happen to the demand for coal, if oil prices drop by 10 per cent?'; quite another to answer the wider question 'what will happen to the demand for coal in five years' time?' And when one comes to many policy decisions, it is questions of this latter kind that demand an answer. Someone has to decide whether the National Coal Board should plan for more or less coal production; and who should be expected to provide the answers if not the economists?

It is here that the trouble begins. For while the economist may be able to list the main factors which will determine the demand for coal (its price in relation to other fuels, the rate of increase in production in those industries using coal, changes in fuel efficiency, the level of consumers' income, etc.), he cannot at present translate this into an answer to the main question, without making assumptions about movements in these factors. And then the answer merely reveals the implications of the assumptions he makes. The appropriate assumptions to make in any given set of circumstances are frequently a matter of judgment, so that two economists, equally technically skilled as economists, might make different assumptions, and, therefore, arrive at different answers.

Again, while the economist may be able to analyse the relation between income, production and expenditure in some past period, and show the importance of this relation in the future, he is on much more uncertain ground when trying to answer the question 'what is going to happen to expenditure in the next twelve months?'. And it is to this question that the public wants an answer in arguing how the government should attempt, through its various policies, to influence the level of expenditure. Expenditure can be considered separately in its various constituents—stock-building, fixed investment, consumption, government expenditure, and exports, and one may be able to assess reasonably reliably what is likely to happen to some of these. But for two crucial ones, stock-building and exports, one is thrown back on exploring what would happen on the basis of alternative assumptions. Answering the further question, what effect particular measures taken by the government to influence expenditure will in fact have, raises a host of further complications. Here is plenty of room for different economists, using different assumptions, to come to different conclusions, even though the general theoretical framework within which they are conducting their analysis is much the same.

It might be argued, and I have frequently argued this way myself, that in such circumstances the economist should emphasize the importance of the assumptions, and the implications of each assumption, rather than the final answer. Let the public and the decision-makers then select which combination of assumptions they think most appropriate. But this will not do. For the public are not good judges of assumptions, and in any case are interested in conclusions, not assumptions. Whenever I have tried to explain important problems of economic policy in this way, I have usually been accused by my audience of trying to evade the issue. 'To explain that the problem is difficult and complex, that it raises questions to which one cannot give a definite answer, is all very well', they say, 'but what would *you do* if you had to decide?' Is it just cowardice and academic escapism to say 'I do not know'? For taking decisions in such circumstances is not merely a matter of judgment about appropriate assumptions, but necessarily implies taking risks, and discussing and analysing the risks involved is quite different from actually having to decide. One can see this quite clearly when academics, including economists, are faced with decision taking in their own affairs in the universities. They may be willing to take bold decisions vicariously about major issues of economic policy, but they rarely show such incisiveness and courage on academic issues.

The problem of policy is, of course, not merely whether the government should encourage or discourage expenditure, but by what means this should be done; by monetary or fiscal policy? and if by fiscal policy, which items of expenditure or taxation should be changed? Here we are right in the middle of political issues. The need to distinguish between the economic and political element in any prescription is emphasized in academic economics, but when economists debate in public they frequently ignore this distinction. In any case the public is interested in what the economist has to say *qua* economist, and cannot be expected to draw fine distinctions about which hat he is wearing when he makes some statement on economic policy. The public cannot be expected to discover for itself whether conflicting prescriptions put forward by economists reflect differences in economic diagnoses, or differences in political views and attitudes. Unless economists are prepared to exercise restraint in expressing views which are largely political, they must not be surprised if their economic arguments are frequently dismissed by the public as part of the political game.

VI

What about the issues which I referred to earlier, where there is still fundamental disagreement between economists themselves? Take, for example, two major problems of current importance, the effect of monopoly or inflation on economic growth. In each case one can make an imposing list of factors pulling in opposing directions. The large firm in a semi-monopolistic position, it can be argued, is an important vehicle of progress because of its capacity and willingness to spend large sums on research and development, and because of its willingness to take risks in innovation, since its position is basically secure. Against this, it can be objected that monopoly is an impediment to progress because absence of competition leads to sluggishness, and large scale implies inefficient bureaucratic control which stifles new ideas. Or on inflation, one can argue that a mildly rising price level gives businessmen the confidence which comes with an apparently ever-expanding market, and provides the necessary incentive for expansion, innovation and risk-taking. Or, in opposition to this, one can argue that inflation leads to insecurity, distortion in production, inhibits saving, makes life too easy for business, and that, in any case, it cannot remain mild for long, but will develop into a destructive runaway price rise.

How choose between these two sets of arguments in each

case? Is it not true that both sets contain elements of truth, and that the really difficult problem is to discover what weight to attach to each in any particular situation? Would not economists' views command greater respect, and therefore more truly educate the public in the issues involved, if they laid greater stress on the difficulty of coming to conclusions of general and universal validity, rather than ranged themselves in opposing schools, each, like mediaeval theologians in disputation, being quite certain that they have the answer?

Here again the fault is partly the public's, partly the economists'. For decisions about monopoly policy and the control of inflation have to be taken, and the public clamours for guidance. If economists merely express agnosticism about the issues involved, others, working with economic ideas picked up in the strangest of ways, will not hesitate to prescribe and advocate particular policies.

The economist may be tempted to stress one set of arguments because he believes this supports a policy which is desirable in any case for other reasons. Take the control of inflation. If, for example, one believes that inflation leads to chronic balance of payments difficulties, and that these in turn weaken the international political and economic influence of the United Kingdom which one would like to see strengthened, how tempting to stress those sides of the argument which would lead to the conclusion that inflation is damaging for domestic economic development as well. And it is because economists so frequently succumb to this kind of temptation that their views on policy are so divergent and conflicting.

VII

Most of my argument has been related to the role of economics and economists in prescribing and discussing policies which are the responsibility of the government. Much of it applies, however, to economists employed by business. A full discussion of the special features of the role that the economist plays in business is beyond the scope of this article and only a brief comment is possible here.

In the large firm the economist may play three roles. First, he may be concerned with explaining what is happening and likely to happen in the general economic situation, what the public debate on economic policy is about, and what action the government is likely to take and why. Since so much of this argument is conducted in the jargon of economics and economic statistics, this explanation of what is going on outside can be given only by an economist.

The usefulness of this activity to the firm itself will vary a great deal. It may merely give the Chairman or Managing Director some element of understanding of the general economic scene, enable him to refer to government policy in his annual speech without making howlers, and guard him from being completely puzzled and taken by surprise by changes in government economic policy. But it may have more direct relevance and application to important decisions on such issues as the firm's investment plans, inventory and pricing policy. Interpretations of economic events abroad, especially where the firm has wide international ramifications either through foreign trade or overseas subsidiaries and branches, may also play an important role. In this more direct use of general analysis of the economic scene, the economist in business uses very much the same kind of mixture of simple theory, economic commonsense and knowledge of facts as his counterpart arguing about public policy. In some firms he may be quite close to actual decision-taking and quickly become aware of the limitations of the usefulness of general economic theory; in others he may be in a remote economic division writing appreciations and analyses which have little effective influence on the operations of the firm.

Secondly, the economist may be concerned with the application of the rapidly developing techniques in statistical and operational analysis, many of which have become relevant to actual business problems, through the use of electronic computers. A whole new field is being opened up here, much of it accessible only to the specialist economic statistician or mathematician, and a closed book to the general economist. The role which these new developments can play in business and the relation between them and the work of the economist, are really outside the main theme of this article.

Lastly, there is the part that someone with a training in economics may play directly in running the business, and it is here that the small or medium-sized firm comes into the picture as well. Here economics is not being used to interpret external economic trends and their likely impact on the firm, or as a technique to get the solution of a specific problem, but as a way of thinking in dealing with internal problems and decisions. This way of thinking is quite distinct from that of the accountant, the engineer, the scientist, or the administrator. It is not easy to specify its content, but it is closely related to notions of logical choice and of tracing the implications of alternative lines of action which are so central to economics. A training in this way of thinking does not by itself make anyone a good businessman, but if someone has the right qualities, whatever they may be, for dealing with business problems, a training in economics may enable him to use these more efficiently.

VIII

The main theme of this article has been that the contribution economics can make to public discussion and policy, although important, is limited. I have argued that there are many complex problems of policy to which the economist does not know the answer, and that many of these involve issues of politics on which the economist is no more competent than anyone else to pass judgment. On such questions there might be more understanding by the public of the issues involved if economists exercised self-restraint and confined themselves to attempting to explain the nature and complexity of the problems, rather than providing conflicting and widely divergent solutions. If such a view of the role of economics and the economist is to gain any acceptance it would mean a radical change, not only in what the public demands of the economist, but also in the way in which economics is taught. For, even at the elementary stage, the student is now frequently led to believe that, were it not for pressure politics, grasping businessmen, cowardly, selfish and ignorant politicians, stupid trade unionists, and the perversemess and obtuseness of the public, economic problems could easily be solved. How often is the student of economics now asked in an examination question, to which he is expected to devote half an hour, to solve the problem of inflation, to settle the future of the sterling area, or to prescribe a policy for the economic development of an under-developed country. All so easily solved, to judge by the answers!

3

The Case for Investment and Productivity[1]

I

SINCE the end of the war there has been a continuous flow of speeches and articles from economists, journalists and politicians telling the public how important it is to increase productivity in British industry and to have a high rate of investment in order to achieve this. If we do this, we are told, the economic prospect before us is bright and promising, full of hope for a continuously rising standard of living; but if we don't, we shall be in a perpetual state of economic crisis, ever on the verge of economic bankruptcy.

Very often when the need for productivity increases and investment is explained, the arguments used imply that there is a critical rate of increase; that if we achieve this rate all will be well, but if we fall below it we shall be in recurrent difficulty. This view is frequently expressed in the literature which the British Productivity Council puts out to British industry. 'The British standard of living cannot be maintained, let alone improved', the Productivity Council states in an outline of its objectives, 'unless our productive efficiency keeps pace with that of other countries'. Yet 'we are convinced that Britain can, nevertheless, in due course enjoy a standard of living second to none'. This seems to imply that if we do what is necessary in taking measures to improve productivity we shall have a standard of living rising by 3 or 4 per cent per annum, but that if we do not, we shall have great difficulty in preventing our standard from falling. Intermediate positions, with a slow but still marked rate of improvement, are not envisaged. It is as if we are forced to choose between penury and prosperity, between a rapidly rising standard and a stationary or falling one.

This view, which implies a certain discontinuity in possible rates of economic progress, has a great appeal. For it enables

[1] *Lloyds Bank Review*, October 1955.

the economic problem to be posed to the public in clear black and white. Either we do what the economists and politicians say is necessary and then all will be well; or we neglect their advice and face disaster. Either, by increasing productivity and investment, we raise the standard of living by a substantial rate year by year, or we have no increase at all. Against such a background, it is easy to see how particular rates of progress and investment become accepted as the right ones to go for. In this country the fashionable objectives are a 3 per cent rate of increase in the standard of living, and 20 per cent of the national income devoted to investment.

In this article I try to examine the basis of these views and particularly to see what economic arguments, if any, there are for picking out a particular rate of increase in productivity, or figures of the ratio of investment to national income, as targets of economic policy, whether there is from the economic point of view an 'ideal' rate of progress, or a range of rates, each with its own problems, costs, consequences and advantages. It may be, of course, that although there are no compelling economic arguments pointing to the conclusion that there is only one rate at which we can go forward, yet there may be powerful political reasons why we should prefer a high rather than a low rate of increase in productivity and output.

II

I ignore at this stage the way in which our dependence on foreign trade affects the argument, not because this is unimportant, but merely in the hope that the issues involved will be clearer if we deal with this separately later. If we confine our attention to our internal economic situation then the argument for increasing productivity is largely tautological. Production and consumption are merely two sides of the same coin. Rising real expenditure per head can only come from rising production per head; if production per head increases year by year by 1, 2 or 3 per cent, then expenditure per head can also rise by 1, 2 or 3 per cent. In the short run it may be possible to increase consumption at the expense of investment or other uses of economic resources; but over the long period the rate of growth of the standard of living, if this is measured in the goods and services per head of the population, cannot diverge from the rate of growth in production per head, or productivity. Of course, if one measures productivity in terms of production per head of the working population alone, or in terms of production per man-hour, then there may be some divergence between the movements of productivity and national income per head, because of changes in the ratio of the working population to the total, or in the average number of hours worked.

Clearly a rise in productivity of 3 per cent per annum gives a more rapidly rising standard than a rise of 1 or 2 per cent per annum, but there is here no compelling economic basis for arguing that 3 per cent is the right figure to go for. It may be a striking way of explaining to the public what an annual increase of 3 per cent in the rate of productivity means, to say with the Chancellor of the Exchequer that this would enable us to double the standard of living in the next twenty-five years. But this is a lesson in arithmetic, not in economics. And the laws of compound rates of interest could be illustrated just as well by taking some other rate: to say, for example, that a $2\frac{1}{2}$ per cent rate of increase would mean a doubling of the standard of living in thirty years.

If one looks at the relationship between productivity and the standard of living in this simple way, then for any rate of increase in productivity we care to assume there is a corresponding rate of increase in the standard of living. There is so far no basis for arguing that it is either all or nothing, or that a particular rate of increase is the right one.

This is not to deny the importance of getting people to realize that, in the long run, increases in the standard of living can come only from increased production, that they cannot be obtained through the magic of government manipulation of taxation or subsidies, and that this applies just as much to the volume of public services—health, education, housing and defence—as to private consumption. And if the politicians make up their minds that the public will be discontented if they do not have rising wages, a rising standard of living and increased welfare services, then there is no doubt considerable political justification for them to urge on the public the need to increase productivity. Whether there are grounds for believing that it is 3 per cent per annum that will keep the public happy is quite a different matter.

It can be argued that it is largely ignorance which impedes

a high rate of increase in productivity, that if managers and workers alike could be made aware more quickly of improved and more up to date methods of production, progress would be much more rapid. But where increasing productivity involves such changes in organization, traditional habits and customary methods of work, as to create social disturbance and the breakdown of old patterns of living, the position is not so clear. Who is to say that the cost is worth paying? There is certainly plenty of room for difference of opinion here, as one can see, for example, by reading the speeches in the recent debate in the House of Commons on the report of the Monopolies Commission. The economist is inclined to argue that the temporary disruption is worth while if in the long run it leads to increases in productivity and the standard of living. The whole tradition of economic thinking sets a high value on material progress. One can argue at great length about the cost and advantages of more or less rapid rates of economic progress without getting very far. For even if we know with reasonable reliability what the costs and advantages are, there is no agreed basis for weighing one against the other. Certainly, there is no economic argument which points to the conclusion that with a 3 per cent rate of increase the benefits balance the costs, and that at any lower rate the benefits clearly predominate.

III

The case for a high rate of investment is mainly based on the need to invest in order to raise productivity and the standard of living. Of course, if we pick on a particular long-run rate of increase in the standard of living as the desirable one, it is in theory possible to say that we must devote some particular proportion of our resources to investment, otherwise the increase will not be achieved. In practice, even so, we cannot say with any reliability in quantitative terms what the necessary relation is between investment and particular rates of increase in productivity and production. We can get little further than 'saying' that increased investment will make for a more rapid rate of increase in output. We benefit from the investment of the past, and the more we invest now, the greater the material benefits we provide for ourselves and generations in the future.

A diversion of more resources to investment involves less consumption of public services now. By what criteria do we decide, as a nation, how much jam we should give up today in exchange for the promise of more jam tomorrow? Suppose we knew, for example, that devoting 20 per cent of the national resources to investment (and leaving 80 per cent for consumption and public services) would yield a 3 per cent rate of increase in productivity in the long run, whereas to devote only 15 per cent to investment (leaving 85 per cent for the other uses) would yield only a 2 per cent increase. How do we choose between the two? When investment depended mainly on the savings of the rich there seemed to be a strong case for urging them to save and invest rather than to engage in profligate personal expenditure, since such investment would benefit the mass of the population in the long run. But now a high rate of saving and investment means a restriction of consumption for a much wider section of the population, and the argument is not so obvious.

No doubt some people would contend that the 'natural' rate of interest, balancing the demand for and supply of savings, would secure the 'right' rate of investment for the country as a whole. The relation between the actual rate of interest and such a 'natural' rate and the effect of the rate of interest on investment, are matters which raise controversial issues outside the scope of this article. In any case such an argument is not really relevant to the point I am trying to make. For it still leaves open the question whether we should take special action to increase the supply of savings by education, propaganda and budgetary policy and to increase the willingness to invest by special taxation and other provisions favouring investment, and by manipulating the rate of interest through monetary policy.

Frequently it is contended that we need a high rate of saving and investment in order to take advantage of the promising technical innovations that rapidly advancing science produces in ever increasing flow; and that the provision to a wider and wider public of new and ever changing consumer goods—cars, refrigerators, washing machines, television sets, and so on—demands more and more capital equipment. In part, this is no more than a special case of the more general argument that we must have a high rate of investment in order to have a high rate of increase in standards of living in the future. In so far as technical innovation by itself is going to lead to increased productivity and higher living standards anyway, it can be taken as an argument both for and against higher investment. For when technical innovation is rapid the opportunities for investment are greater and the returns from investment are higher; and this makes investment more attractive. But our reaction to such rosy prospects for the future, may be a willingness to forgo less, rather than more, from our present standards. If our children are going to have the benefits of atomic power, automatic factories, and other yet unheard of industrial miracles, why should we strain ourselves now in order to add yet further to their standards? If we are really on the verge of a new industrial revolution with great potentialities for increasing productivity, is it really vital to push up investment now? Cannot we take advantage of the great new opportunities a little more slowly?

Some people would argue that an intermediate rate of innovation is not really possible. On the one hand, you may have a business community that is energetic, adventurous, anxious to take risks, seizing every opportunity for increasing efficiency; such a business community will not be satisfied with a slow rate of innovation. And a society which produces such a business community is likely to be one which puts a high value on material progress and, therefore, one in which workers are also willing—indeed anxious—to accept new techniques and methods of production which give them a higher standard of living. On the other hand, the business community and workers alike may be bound by tradition and customary ways of doing things, unwilling to consider new methods and ideas, and taking little interest in new techniques and new products. Between the two, it may be argued, there are no stable intermediate stages: a society may have periods of rapid innovation and economic development or periods of stagnation, but slow gradual increase is rare. This is a view which one cannot easily substantiate or refute. At first sight, it is hardly supported by the experience of the United Kingdom in the last fifty years, where there has been a sluggish but still quite definite rate of increase in productivity and a continuous if not spectacular rate of innovation.

The case for high investment is often supported by point-ing to the poor state of existing capital in this country: for example, the railways and the roads. And perhaps it is true that in relation to other items of capital expenditure, such as housing, too little has been spent on these in the post-war period. But this raises the issue of the right distribution of investment, rather than its general level.

There is also the argument that a high rate of investment is necessary to keep the economy fully employed; that without it resources would be idle and labour unemployed. In such circumstances investment is all benefit; there is no question of weighing up jam today against more jam tomorrow: we have both. This was a fashionable and perhaps relevant argument in the 1930's and it still apparently plays some role in econo-mic discussion in the United States; but it has little bearing on the economic situation in this country since the war.

IV

If we regard our internal economic situation only, therefore, there seem to be no clear compelling economic reasons why we should pursue a high rate of increase in productivity and devote a substantial proportion of our resources to invest-ment. Our policy and actions, both individually and collec-tively, could be related simply to the value that we place on a rising standard of living, and how far we are prepared to forgo benefits now in order to enjoy higher standards later. How does our dependence on foreign trade complicate and alter the position? It is, of course, usually argued that what-ever choice we might have otherwise, the need to compete overseas compels us to take measures to increase our effi-ciency and productivity and to undertake the investment which is necessary for this. Otherwise we shall be in continuous difficulty in competing in export markets, will be unable to buy the food and raw materials that we want, and will be in chronic balance of payments difficulty.

Our competitive position overseas depends to a substantial degree on the prices that we charge compared with other suppliers. Prices of final products are a function of raw material prices, wage rates and other costs, as well as of changes in productivity. Over imported raw materials costs we have little control, but we can hope that in the long run we do not have to pay any higher prices than our main competitors. For the other factors, the higher the level of productivity in relation to money rates, the lower the level of prices. It is the combination of the two that is crucial. In the case of labour, for example, the combination of the movement in money wage rates or money earnings and labour productivity. What matters is the effect of the two together on prices in relation to those of our competitors. If productivity in export industries here and in the USA is increasing by, say, 4 per cent per annum, while wage rates here are increasing by 6 per cent and in the USA by 4 per cent, inevitably our prices will become less competitive.

The competitiveness of our exports depends, therefore, not only on the rate of increase in productivity here, but also on the rate of change in wage, salary and other money income compared with that occurring overseas. Our monetary policy has to be geared closely to events overseas. If our main competitors, USA and Germany, are going through an inflationary phase, with incomes and prices rising substantially, we can afford, if we wish, to allow the same to happen here. But if they are keeping their prices, especially their export prices, stable, whereas we allow our money incomes, especially in export industries, to rise more than the increase in productivity, we are courting trouble. Relative movements in productivity are clearly an important element in the situation, though not necessarily the most important. We cannot escape for long from keeping our monetary policy in line with that of other countries, by pressing for greater increases in productivity. No doubt, if money incomes here are increasing by 3 per cent, the problem of maintaining our position in export markets is easier if productivity is increasing by 3 per cent rather than by 2 per cent or not at all. But there is no magic in the rate of 3 per cent; there is no guarantee that at this rate money incomes will rise no more than productivity, and that our export prices will be at the right level compared with those of other countries.

It can indeed be argued that the very circumstances which are conducive to a high rate of increase in productivity are themselves likely to lead to money incomes rising even faster and to our prices becoming too high—unless, of course, the same forces are also in operation in the economies of our competitors. Suppose it were true that workers will agree to the introduction of new techniques and new labour saving methods of production, which are a necessary condition of a high rate of increase in productivity, only if there is so high a level of employment as to produce an acute shortage of labour. Suppose also that businessmen will not invest at a high rate and explore new ways of increasing output and efficiency unless they see a guaranteed and expanding market for their output. Suppose, in other words, that conditions of inflation or near inflation are necessary to get a high rate of increase in productivity. It is because they take this view that many people regard mild inflation with favour. But these are the very conditions which make it easy for everyone to demand increases in money incomes beyond the increases taking place in productivity, and which give an upward twist to our export prices. They are also the circumstances in which demand in the home market is so great that exporting, usually more troublesome and risky, is neglected. So that although a high rate of increase in productivity may appear to help to keep us competitive overseas, if such an increase can only be secured at the cost of continuous inflation, the advantage overseas may, in the short run at least, be more than offset by the other consequences of such inflation.

Pressure for a high rate of home investment may have similar consequences. In the long run it may mean increased efficiency and competitiveness overseas. But in the short run pressure for increased investment at home, especially if it is accompanied by an easy budget policy, itself adds fuel to the inflationary forces. And many of the goods needed in industrial investment, especially engineering products, are among those which are easiest to sell abroad. It is hardly surprising, therefore, that at times of incipient balance of payments trouble, the official pressure urging more investment is relaxed; indeed, that there is often even an attempt to go into reverse. Rarely at such times does one hear the argument that we should invest more, in order to increase productivity still further and so make exports more competitive.

It is the whole set of forces which influence the incentive to export and our export prices in relation to those of our competitors that need to be watched. To pick out productivity or investment and concentrate attention on these at the expense of everything else will merely mislead us. If a near-inflationary situation at home, with negligible unemployment, is a condition of a high rate of increase in productivity, then this will aggravate rather than alleviate our overseas position, at least in the short run.

International comparisons of movements in money costs, prices and productivity are extremely difficult to make. The following table shows the movement in money wage rates and export prices of manufactures for the United States, Germany and the United Kingdom since 1950. The figures have to be used with great caution. There are no indices of wage rates for the United States and Germany, and the figures of hourly earnings are affected by the changing amount of work at overtime rates, variations in piece rates, as well as shifts in employment. The composition of trade in manufactures is different for the three countries and this affects the movement in the indices of average values.

WAGES AND EXPORT PRICES IN UK, USA, AND GERMANY
1950 = 100

	United Kingdom			United States		Germany	
		†			Export	Av. Hourly	Export
		Av. Hourly	Export	Av. Hourly	Av. Value	Earnings in	Av. Value
	Weekly	Earnings	Av. Value	Earnings	of	Manfctg.	of
	Wage	in	of	in	Finished	and	Finished
	Rates	Manfctg.	Manfcts.	Manfctg.	Manfcts.	Building	Products
1951	108	108	117	109	111	115	115
1952	117	119	125	114	112	124	126
1953	123	125	122	121	112	129	125
1954	128	132	119	124	113	132	121
1955	137*	143	121*	128‡	112‡	137§	122§

* June   † April each year   ‡ May   § First quarter

In the period of the Korean boom, which was still to some extent a period of adjustment to the effects of devaluation in the United Kingdom, wage rates and export prices rose more in Germany and the United Kingdom than in the United States. During this period the United Kingdom used up a substantial part of the price advantage over the United States that was obtained by the 1949 devaluation of sterling. From 1952 to 1954, however, export prices were steady in all three countries. The remarkable stability in prices of United Kingdom manufactures is confirmed by the Board of

Trade new index of the wholesale price of manufactured products. This rose steeply from 103 (June 1949 = 100) in January 1950 to 129·6 in March 1952, and then remained stable until the end of 1954 (126·3).

Wage rates in the United Kingdom have taken a leap forward since the beginning of 1955, and by June were already 5½ per cent higher than at the end of 1954. There is no evidence that current increases in productivity are sufficient to absorb such wage increases without affecting prices. The index number of prices of exports of manufactures has increased by 2 per cent in the first six months of this year, the main increase being in the index for metals; and the wholesale price index of manufactured products began to move up appreciably from the beginning of the year (by 2 per cent to June). But it is not easy to tell how far this is a reflection of wage increases and how far the delayed effect of imported raw material prices, some of which—for example, those of non-ferrous metals—have risen markedly since the beginning of 1954. The effects of these movements on the competitiveness of British prices depends a good deal on whether there is similar wage pressure in the United States and Germany. So far this year the increases in those two countries seem to have been on a smaller scale than in this country.

v

The last section was mainly concerned with the effects in the short run of pressure to increase productivity and have a high rate of investment on our competitive position abroad and the stability of the balance of payments. If we attempt a longer run view, the conclusion we come to depends on the assumptions we make about the various forces at work; and we can have as many different conclusions as combinations of assumptions we care to take.

Only a combination of all the most gloomy and pessimistic assumptions would lead to the conclusion that in the long run 'the British standard of living cannot be maintained, let alone improved, unless our productive efficiency keeps pace with that of other nations'. Such a statement implies that our competitors use rising efficiency in their export industries mainly to reduce their prices, and take little of the benefit in rising money incomes to those engaged in these industries; as a consequence, to maintain our exports, we should have to re-duce our prices too. If our productivity is not rising as much as that of our competitors, we could do this only by reducing money incomes or by progressive devaluation. If we assume that at the same time there is little or no increase in pro-ductivity in food and raw materials production, and that the relation between world demand and supply results in ever increasing difficulty in our getting imports, then we should also be faced with the prospect of having to pay higher and higher prices for our imports. Such an adverse movement in the terms of trade could theoretically be sufficiently large to offset completely rising productivity here, so that we should need substantial increases in productivity merely to prevent our standard of living from falling. We should have to run faster and faster merely to stay in the same place.

I cannot see that there is evidence for taking such an extremely gloomy view of the future. If there were, all talk of doubling our standard of living in twenty-five years would be miserable deception; for the unfavourable forces implied in these assumptions do not disappear if we have increasing productivity at 3 per cent per annum rather than 1 or 2 per cent per annum, or if we devote 20 per cent of the national income to investment rather than 15 per cent.

The long-run problem of competing overseas may rein-force the need for high investment, especially in export in-dustries, from a different point of view. Over the years, competitiveness in price, which we might be able to secure by restraining the rise in money incomes here or by manipu-lating the exchange rate, may not be enough. If our competi-tors, through technical advance and innovation, are offering new products, we are not likely to be able to sell goods which are out of date, even if these are relatively cheaper. In many markets, especially for machinery and equipment, it is superiority in operation and design, rather than difference in price, which affects the volume of sales. And we can only hope to be able to offer the most up to date products, the argument runs, if we have a rapid rate of technical and pro-duct innovation at home, which in turn is not possible with-out substantial investment in manufacturing industry. This is a powerful argument for keeping innovation here abreast of that of our main competitors. But it is as well to keep in mind that in fact the needs of investment in the export industries are only a small part of total investment, and that even here it is hardly a question of all or nothing.

If we have a high rate of increase in productivity and investment, will it help the balance of payments in the long run? Here again the answer depends on the assumptions one makes. At first glance it is difficult to imagine that it could do other than help. But there are some who would argue that given our heavy dependence on imports for food and raw materials, rising production and incomes in this country may make our underlying balance of payments progressively more difficult. As our production increases, it is argued, we shall have to import more raw materials and as our incomes increase we shall want to import more food. If at the same time world trade in manufactures is not growing at a sufficiently rapid rate, we may find chronic difficulty in expanding the volume of our exports. On this view, the more successful we are in the long run in raising production at home, the higher the level of foreign trade, both imports and exports, which will be required and the more difficult it will be to secure this. As with many other arguments in this field, it is difficult to produce the evidence either to substantiate or refute this view. But the fact that it should be held at all at least serves to illustrate the point that there are no obviously compelling balance of payments arguments which point to the need for rapidly increasing production and productivity.

VI

The economic arguments for a high rate of investment and rate of increase in productivity prove thus to be neither simple nor obvious. And it is hardly surprising, therefore, that those who support the case for productivity frequently fall back on political arguments. The line of reasoning is very familiar. For reasons of international prestige and in order to maintain our standing in the world we must keep abreast of the other leading nations in the economic race. Other countries, especially the backward areas of the world, will be much more impressed by the British way of doing things if they see that we have a standard of living rising as rapidly as that of any other country. Rising productivity here will make it easier for us to contribute to the economic development of such backward areas, and this is desirable on humanitarian as well as political grounds. With higher production per head we shall no longer need to rely on the United States for contributions to our defence, and so will avoid the embarrassment of appearing to be committed by such aid to supporting United States policy. With greater wealth we will in any case be able to spend more on defence should this be necessary, and if we make a greater contribution to the defence of the West we can expect more notice to be taken of our views in international political negotiations. Such arguments, and many others on similar lines, seem to provide a more powerful and straightforward basis for urging the need for increased productivity and a high rate of investment than any economic argument. For in essence the economic argument amounts to little more than saying that if we want a rising standard of living we must do what is necessary to achieve a rising volume of output.

4

Economic Planning in War and Peace[1]

To attempt within the compass of a single paper to deal with this difficult and complex subject inevitably results in my concentrating on particular aspects of the problem which interest me, at the expense of only summary mention of others which some of you will consider to be of equal importance. I also feel considerable hesitation in raising in this paper issues which are inevitably the subject of political controversy, although I may attempt to excuse my action to some extent on the grounds that I do not feel that the division on these issues follows party lines. I am emboldened to put my views on this subject, principally because I feel that the current popularity of the view that the Government must accept responsibility for planning the use of the economic resources of the country in peace-time, arises from a mistaken analogy of the essential nature of the economic problem in war and peace, and an erroneous view of the nature of Government economic planning in war-time and the processes by which it was operated. We hear so often in current discussion the problem of economic planning dismissed with a statement such as: 'The Government planned the use of our economic resources successfully during the war, why shouldn't it be able to do so equally successfully in peace-time?' Now this rhetorical question implies three assumptions. Firstly, that the essential function of economic planning is the same in war and peace; secondly, that we did by some criterion (the one usually used is that we won the war, which I don't accept as valid) plan successfully, and thirdly that the main instruments and methods of planning which were used during the war are available and appropriate for use in peace-time. It is with the first and last of these three assumptions that I shall be mainly concerned in this paper.

Why was planning accepted as both inevitable and desir-

[1] Paper read to the Manchester Statistical Society, November 1947.

able during the war? If we can find the answer to this question we shall have discovered the essential nature of the war-time problem which planning attempted to solve. For it is one of the striking features of the current planning controversy, in this country at least, that whatever differences of view there may be about the advisability of what for want of a better term is called 'physical planning' by the Government in peace-time, all parties to the dispute are agreed that such planning was necessary during the war.

The prime objective of economic policy in war-time was to secure the transfer of the maximum volume of resources to the war sector of the economy in the shortest possible time. This objective could in my view only be achieved by a financial policy which was inevitably inflationary. The Government had, therefore, to introduce control and restrictions on the use of private income and business resources in order to prevent runaway inflation, which all are agreed would have resulted in a complete breakdown of the economic system. Now it is possible to argue that such a transfer could have been secured equally speedily by means of a financial policy which was not inflationary. Although I am not foolish enough to assert that our financial policy was perfect in all respects, I am prepared to maintain that we could not have operated successfully a non-inflationary financial policy.

My main arguments for this view are, first, that the technical financial problems of raising the whole of Government expenditure during the war by taxation or voluntary saving, in a system where the use of resources was left free, would have been insuperable. Secondly, in the early stages of the war the transfer of resources from peace-time to war-time uses depended principally on the favourable price and wage differentials as between the war and peace sectors. Such differentials were immeasurably easier to secure in a system where all prices were rising but where the price rise was greater in the war than in the peace sector, than it would have been in a system where the general level of prices changed little, but where the differential had to be secured by depressing prices in the peace sector and increasing prices in the war sector. Thirdly, the successful operation of such a non-inflationary policy would have involved the Government in calculating with precision the technical possibilities of transferring resources to the war economy year by year or even month by month; and so adjusting its taxation policy as to secure that what was left in the pockets of consumers was just sufficient to buy what remained in the non-war sector, while the proceeds of taxation and savings were just sufficient to pay for the products of the war sector. Such a nice calculation would have been beyond the capacities of the best brains in the Government service or of those of the many outside experts who were so readily prepared to give advice. It would also have implied a degree of flexibility and almost day to day adjustments in taxation that was unattainable and would in any case have been most trying and confusing to those who would have had to attempt to operate it. The Government could only operate by exerting the maximum financial pressure, and then plugging by physical control the inflationary gaps as it saw them arising in actual experience.

But whether the Government operated through an inflationary or non-inflationary policy, it would have been unable to operate solely through the medium of the creation of price differentials between the war and non-war sectors. For under either financial policy, the margin of difference in price that would have been necessary in order to secure such a large turnover of resources would have been very wide, and would have resulted in the accrual of large windfall gains in income to those who were in the position of possessing resources of use in the war sector of the economy. For political reasons the Government was forced to offset such gains by taxation; and, in so far as this policy was successful, it necessarily blunted the incentive to resources to move from the peace to the war sector, and frustrated the whole policy of operating through the price mechanism.

In order to proceed to the next stage of my argument, let us now suppose that none of these difficulties had arisen, or that they were capable of solution without resort to administrative planning and control. I would then like to put to you my second argument why the necessary expansion in war production would not have taken place. This expansion required investment on a large scale in new factories and machines specifically designed for the production of weapons of war and of little or negligible use for any other purpose. There is surely every reason for believing that business men would not have been prepared to undertake the risks involved in such investment. For they had no basis on which they could assess the likely length of the war or the tactics and strategy that would be used in its conduct. And for obvious reasons of military secrecy, it would have been quite impossible to have made the views of the Government and the Services on these questions available to the whole business community. But even if business men had been prepared to undertake such risks, would they have been competent to do so? Is there any reason for believing that out of the multiplicity of individual investment decisions taken by business men, the best allocation of resources for prosecuting the war would have been secured? If business men had been prepared to undertake the risks involved, the process of operating through the market mechanism would then have worked by business men discovering in the event that some investments were profitable and others unprofitable, and competition would have resulted in the curtailment of the unprofitable and the expansion of the profitable investments. But since much of war-time investment was long term, this process of selection would have taken far too long and was in any case wasteful if there were other obviously more reliable methods of choosing the most useful avenues of investment. And I maintain that Government Departments and the Services were best able to decide which were the most profitable lines of investment from the point of view of the successful prosecution of the war.

Captal investment had, therefore, to be directly financed or underwritten by the Government. The exercise of this function alone would have led Government Departments right into the centre of the whole field of physical planning. For this involved decisions not only as to rate of investment necessary for a given monthly output of the final product, but also as to the form the investment should take—which implied which methods of production should be used—and the choice of firms who should undertake the investment. And it was not sufficient for the Government to undertake the investment necessary in the final stages of production (e.g. for the assembly of Spitfires and Hurricanes); it had also to undertake the investment necessary for the manufacture of components and raw materials (e.g. aero engines, radio equipment and aluminium fabricating capacity). For the business man was just as unwilling and incompetent to decide what risks should be taken in the investment in components and raw materials as in investment for the production of the final weapons of war.

Such decisions about investment in component and raw materials production led Government Departments into the other main aspect of planning, Given that it was necessary for the Government to decide not only the rate of investment in and hence the rate of production of the final weapons of war, but also the rate of investment in and the rate of production of the components and raw materials needed for those final products, it had to secure the co-ordination of these various rates of investment and production. To ensure, for example, that the capacity laid down for the production of propellers would give sufficient propellers for the aircraft that it was planned to produce. And where the raw materials concerned were of use in the non-war as well as the war sector of the economy the decision as to the investment necessary, implied not only a view of the rate of production needed for weapons of war but also of the rate of supplies which would be required or would be allowed for the non-war sector.

This leads me to the third argument which I wish to put forward for the necessity and desirability of detailed physical planning by Government Departments in war-time. It is this third argument that I regard as fundamental, for the two arguments I have already put forward are in my view merely special cases of this more general one. During the war the community entrusted to the Government, and through them to the fighting services, the responsibility for deciding on the best and most efficient methods of fighting the war. The war was conducted on the assumption that there was always a best way of fighting and that it was the duty of the Government and the Service Departments to find that best way. The community was, so to speak, trying to act as a single individual who attempts to choose the way in which he can best use the resources available to him in order to achieve a single objective. If the community attempts to act in this way as a single individual then is must leave to the Government the decision as to how that single objective can best be achieved.

If we are agreed on this, then I feel that the necessity for the whole apparatus of central planning in war-time inevitably

E

follows. For I can see no way in which the Government can then avoid the task of deciding the best use of the resources, by throwing the responsibility on to the market mechanism. One of the principal functions of the market mechanism is to resolve the conflict of individuals each seeking their own, although not necessarily selfish, objectives. It would, of course, have been possible for the war to have been waged on such principles; for each individual or associations of individuals to have decided how they thought the war would best be waged, and for them then to use the resources which they commanded to see that those weapons would be produced which they thought most useful. It is possible that through the process of this conflict between individuals singly and in groups—the failure of those who were wrong and the success of those who were right—that the best method of fighting the war would have emerged; always provided, of course, that the enemy would have been prepared to regard all this as a trial process and would have promised not to defeat us in the meantime. Unless we take the view that this would have been a better way of fighting the war, then we must acknowledge that the reconciliation of views as to the best way of conducting the war had to be decided before and not after the allocation of resources had been fixed, and that this was a responsibility which the Government alone could assume. For it was the Government which had to decide on the minimum standard of living which the population must enjoy in order to maintain its efficiency as a producing machine (for in war-time the citizens outside the Armed Forces were principally regarded, and quite rightly, as another factor of production). The Government had to choose what combination of Army, Navy and Air Force, what combination of tanks, guns, aircraft and battleships, would give the optimum fighting power in relation to the expected strategy of the enemy.

Now this means that there is an inevitable tendency all the time to centralize to the maximum degree possible the decisions as to what shall be produced, for it is only by such centralization that the fitting of each action into the single objective as interpreted by the Government can be achieved. For each weapon must be considered in its usefulness in relation to all others, and in relation to all the alternative uses to which the resources used in its production could be put. I can see no way in which the choice between guns and tanks, men in the Armed Forces or increased munitions production, could be thrown on to the market mechanism.

I have heard it argued that although the choice between final products had to be made by the Government and that the market mechanism cannot absolve the Government from deciding what particular collection of weapons it wants for fighting the war, that this is as far as the planning process needs to be taken in war-time; and that the optimum allocation of components and raw materials for those final products could have been secured more easily through the operation of a market mechanism than through planning and allocation systems. Now I have already argued, and I think that the argument is conclusive, that the investment decisions as to the capacity needed for different components and materials had to be taken by the Government and that as a consequence the Government had to decide what rates of production of components and materials were appropriate to its plans for the production of the final weapons of war. (These two sets of decisions are, of course, not independent; for the plans for the production of the final weapons would be in part determined by the availability of components and materials, so that in theory the two sets of decisions were really one and had to be taken together.) The argument is, therefore, reduced to the desirability of operating through the price mechanism in order to secure the allocation between different uses of capacity already planned, and the distribution of output when produced.

Let us try to see how such a system might have worked in aircraft production. The Ministry of Aircraft Production would have determined and financed the capital expenditure necessary for aircraft, component, equipment and raw material production; would have placed contracts for complete aircraft; and would have then have left aircraft manufacturers to compete with one another in the market for the supplies of components, equipment and raw materials which they needed. Let us ignore for the moment the possibilities of such a system leading to inflation, to the exploitation of the position by manufacturers in a monopoly position, and the likelihood that undue preference would be given to old standing or potential post-war customers. All of these I submit are not unimportant considerations; I neglect them only so that I can concentrate on what I consider to be the essential issue.

In such a system the pulling power of each aircraft manufacturer on supplies of components and materials, and in turn of each component manufacturer on the supplies and materials which he needed, would depend on the price that he would be prepared to pay, which would in turn depend in part on the price which MAP would be prepared to pay for the aircraft. As each manufacturer tried to get more of the limited supplies of the goods which he needed, he would have bid up the price and would have attempted to pass on the increase in price to MAP. For this system to have worked at all, therefore, it would have been essential for the funds available to MAP to be limited, for otherwise MAP would merely have attempted to get more finance from the Treasury in order to pay the higher prices, and the problem of the allocation of the limited capacity and supplies of components and materials would have remained unsolved.

If its funds were limited, MAP would have had to decide what distribution of expenditure would give the best allocation of resources from the point of view of the Services, and would, therefore, have had to judge of the effects of the particular prices which it offered, not only on the rate of supply it could expect, but also on the quality of the final product. In doing this MAP would have had to weigh up the use of its resources on one line of expenditure compared with another; that, for example, an extra £1,000 for a Spitfire would enable the Spitfire manufacturers to command the best Merlin engines, and a reduction of the price for the Hurricane would have forced manufacturers of the Hurricane to engine their aircraft with second best Merlins. Now I maintain that it was easier for officials in MAP to think in terms of the real alternatives themselves—that they could have all the best engines in Spitfires at the cost of having the second best in Hurricanes—than through the money medium. But, in any case, there is no reason to believe that they would have got the best aircraft/engine combination if they had left this to be determined by competitive bidding by the manufacturers. For although it is true that in the end some manufacturer might have discovered that the difference which MAP was prepared to pay for a Spitfire with a first-class

Merlin as compared with a Spitfire with a second-class Merlin engine more than covered the price of a first-class Merlin, the scope for competition from which such discoveries emerge was so limited, that the process of adjustment would have been extremely slow and painful. And this system would have involved continuous, and often very substantial, changes in the prices which MAP would have been prepared to pay, and business men could not be expected to forecast such changes. In my view they would have been quite unwilling to enter into contracts with their suppliers unless they had some guarantee that their costs would be covered. And if MAP had been prepared to give such guarantees, the competitive price process would have been impossible to operate.

In fact MAP and the Air Ministry insisted, and I feel quite rightly insisted, on determining the aircraft/engine combination which it best preferred. And in order to do this, had not only to plan in detail the programme of the engine manufacturers but also the allocation of their output once produced.

The necessity for doing this derived from the fact that the choice in the use of resources, and the risks implied in that choice, had to be undertaken by the Government and the Services. Since the Government and the Services were attempting to act as a single individual with a single objective in view, they found it easier and simpler to think of each course of action in terms of real choice open to them, than by constructing some system of prices and allocation of money to the various Departments to secure this optimum use of resources. As I see it, this is because the market mechanism is principally of use where it is both necessary and desirable to disperse the taking of decisions, when each individual has to determine what he thinks is best for himself in the light of the circumstances with which he is faced; but that it is of little use where the principal problem is that of delegation, where the objective is to secure that the individual acts not as he thinks best for himself, but that he acts in the way most appropriate to the achievement of an objective which someone superior to him has determined.

I must admit that I am by no means satisfied with the way that I have dealt with this issue, and I have little doubt that you find my explanation even more unsatisfactory than I do myself. I hope you will forgive me if I attempt to illustrate the point I am trying to make by seeing how a small community might act in such circumstances. One could imagine a small community of say one hundred people, each of whom had different capacities and different tastes, and in which the choice as to work and the products to be made was left to the individual, and in which some sort of exchange economy, albeit primitive, would develop and perform a useful function. Now suppose that such a community decided for one reason or another to wage war against another community. Then the point I am making is that such a community would decide as a community how the war should be waged, and how each individual would be most appropriately employed in order to secure the effective prosecution of the war. Even if all the individuals surrendered their income to a leader whom they had chosen he could not operate through a market mechanism, for in allocating money to each individual he would have to ensure that each used that money in the ways in which he, the leader, thought most effective for the prosecution of the war. It would, of course, be possible for each individual to fight the war as he himself thought best, or in association with others who agreed with him, and to use the resources which he possessed, or could obtain through exchange, to further his plans. But then the community would not be fighting as a community but as separate individuals or associations of individuals; and the chances of their being defeated fighting individually would be much greater than if they fought as a community. I maintain that it was because we wished to fight the war as a nation that we were forced to act as this small community would have done; and that the whole process of central control and planning was essential to secure that, as far as possible, each individual's actions were directed towards the ultimate objective of fighting war in the way in which those responsible for its operation thought best.

Finally, I think that planning was necessary in war-time because even if it had been possible to work through the price mechanism, the Government and the general public would have thought, rightly or wrongly that the allocation of resources was being left to 'the blind forces of chance'. The process of turnover of resources from peace to war was inevitably slow, and public impatience at this slowness would have forced the Government to take what appeared to be conscious action to control the course of events. For whatever the disadvantages of planning it does seem to give a feeling, at least to the planners, that the course of events is being consciously controlled.

For all these reasons I conclude that it was both inevitable and desirable that during the war the Government should seek to decide on the uses to which the resources of the community should be put through the medium of planning, control, and rationing in physical terms. It would be quite mistaken, however, to conclude from this that the processes by which Government economic planning operated in war-time, in any way resembled the theoretical structures of the overall planners. I hope you will not think I am misrepresenting these theoretical planners, when I suggest that it is something like the following picture which they usually portray. There is usually a Supreme Planning Board or Being which is provided by the statisticians and technicians (these are usually implicitly assumed to be in unlimited supply) of both the Production and Service Departments with a balance sheet. This shows on one side of the balance a long list of all the resources —the labour, capital, food, and raw materials—available or capable of being made available, and presumably the various alternative combinations in which these resources could be used. On the other side of the sheet is a detailed list of all the requirements of the Service and Civilian Departments—how many air squadrons and airfields the Air Ministry would like to have, how much food is necessary to feed the population, what the Board of Trade thinks the clothes ration ought to be, etc., etc. The Supreme Planning Board then considers the various alternative ways in which the resources can be used and decides, in the light of the single objective of the successful prosecution of the war, on the Grand Plan for the use of these resources. It is true we are never told how long this process of decision takes. This plan then goes out to all concerned as a basis for action, and all lesser plans are derived from it and fit in with it. The Supreme Planning Board remains in continuous session to modify the Grand Plan in the light of changing conditions.

Now this theoretical structure of planning is a complete travesty of the way in which planning operated during the war. And there is quite a simple explanation for this. For such a system presupposes the existence of a race of Supermen who are capable of comprehending in their own minds the interrelation of every variable in the economic system in relation to the innumerable alternative ways in which they could be used, and assumes that the various elements in the economic system can be moved about at will by the Supermen like pawns on a chess-board. Although there does appear among us every now and then a meglomaniac who considers that he belongs to this breed, it is time that we all recognized that such Supermen do not exist. It is indeed the main irony of the problem of war that although the nation must act as far as is possible as one individual, the very limitations of the human mind and capacities prevents the nation from even remotely achieving this objective.

It is out of this conflict between the desirability of acting as a single individual and the limitation of human capacities, that the main practical problem of planning in war-time arises. For on the one hand, in order to secure that all individual action is related as far as possible to the single objective of fighting the war in the way decided by the Government, it is necessary that the taking of decisions should be highly centralized. It is only by centralization that it is possible to ensure that the action of individuals will fit in with each other and will also fit into the desired general pattern. On the other hand, it is an inevitable feature of administration which results from the limitations of human capacity that the more highly centralized the decisions, the more generalized the basis on which they must be taken and the fewer the relationships that can be taken into account. Hence the complaints that the structures of the central planners are academic and are un-related to the real facts of the situation. And so arises the demand for the maximum amount of delegation and decentra-lization in order to secure that action is related to what is really possible. But the greater the degree of decentralization, the more difficult it is to ensure that individual action is really related to the general objective and to take account of all the effects of each action on other factors in the system. The central planner comes to know less and less about more and more, while the man doing the job comes to know more and more about less and less.

The task of planning in war-time is not, therefore, one of finding the perfect method of planning and co-ordination, for this can never be achieved no matter how many planning committees and super-planners and co-ordinators are appointed, but of finding a balance between the two opposing tendencies—the one towards centralization in order to secure the maximum degree of co-ordination, and the other towards decentralization and delegation in order to secure the maximum degree of realism in planning. And the experience of the war showed conclusively that any compromise between these two principles inevitably results in a system of operation which is far from perfect.

In the early years of the war there was little attempt at the central direction of production. As far as I am aware no one worked out, or attempted to work out, what resources would be left after meeting the minimum needs of the civilian population, and how these resources should be divided between the Armed Forces, and the production of aircraft, army and naval supplies. It is true that general decisions were taken about the size of the Army, Air Force, and Navy to plan for, but these decisions were by no means clear cut and did not in any case take account of the interrelation between the size of the Armed Forces and the production of munitions that would be needed for them. Each supply department was left to proceed with its plan for expansion in the light of the requirements that were put to it by the appropriate Service Department. It was only later, as the war proceeded, and these various plans came into conflict that a system of central direction to solve these conflicts was evolved; and by that time the general outlines of the plans of the various departments concerned were already determined, at least for a substantial period of time ahead.

In this process of reconciliation no attempt was ever made to reconcile at one and the same time the plans of the departments in relation to all the factors which affected them. The process of reconciliation took place *seriatim* at different committees, each of which was not always fully aware of the action being taken by the others. Thus there were separate committees for allocating supplies of raw materials, of shipping space, of man-power and of building capacity. It would have been quite impossible for any single committee to have considered at one and the same time the allocation of all these resources, interrelated though they were. As a result not only were the individuals on these committees often out of touch with the latest strategic needs of the war, but they were also out of touch with what the individuals on the other co-ordinating committees were doing.

The main link and co-ordinating mechanism between the various allocating committees was provided by the production programmes of the individual supply departments. It was by the effect on the plans of the individual departments of the decisions of any one of the allocating committees, and the further reaction of these altered plans on the decisions of the other committees, that the whole planning process was kept in motion. Thus, if the man-power committee cut the allocation of labour to the Ministry of Aircraft Production, as a result MAP would reduce its aircraft programme; this would in turn reduce MAP's requirements for steel, timber, building capacity, etc., and these reduced requirements would be taken into account by the appropriate allocating committee at the next quarterly review. It might be that at such a review MAP's steel allocation was cut even further, and this would involve a further readjustment in its programme, which would again have its effects on MAP's demand for other factors. It was indeed only in so far as departments were prepared to alter their programme in accordance with these changing allocations that the system operated at all.

Essentially the same set of problems had to be faced by each department in its own internal planning. It is, for exmaple, quite wrong to think of MAP considering all the various resources available for aircraft production in relation to the demands of the Service Departments, and then drawing up a master plan giving the Service Departments the collection of aircraft most preferred by them out of the various choices open, and showing the production required of each component, equipment, and raw material. This was never done, and could never have been done, unless it had been possible to stop the whole process of production and the war for two or three years while someone worked out the interrelation between all the variable factors in aircraft, component and raw material production, and then decided on the best combination. The most that could be achieved, and even then with great difficulty, was to ensure that the plans for a few of the major components—e.g. the engine, propeller, undercarriage—were co-ordinated with those for the final aircraft, on the assumption that if this relationship was kept straight the other items would adjust themselves fairly easily in practice. When quick decisions about changes in the aircraft programme had to be taken even this degree of co-ordination was impossible; it had to be limited to the relationship of the two most important variables—the airframe and engine.

Even this limited degree of co-ordination could only be achieved by making what were quite unwarrantable assumptions, in order to simplify the problems to be solved. For example, in the man-power budget, where an attempt was made to resolve the conflict of departments in their demands for man-power, the assumption was made that all men and women were alike in their capacities and skill, that labour was equally scarce over all regions of the country and that labour could be moved relatively easily from one employment to another. No one thought these assumptions were in any way related to the facts, but for the man-power committee to have attempted to allocate region by region, according to skill and according to degrees of mobility, would have resulted in the complete breakdown of this attempt at co-ordination. It had, therefore, to work as if these assumptions were correct or to neglect to pay attention to them as relatively unimportant. Again the man-power committee had to assume that each department could calculate with fair accuracy the labour required for any given programme, and that it would not attempt to bluff the committee in order to secure the maximum allocation of labour. In fact, the margin of error in the departmental estimates was often much greater than the changes in the labour allocation under discussion.

Similarly MAP's attempts at internal co-ordination even within the limited sphere mentioned earlier, were far from perfect. For it was impossible to assess with any degree of accuracy the production either of aircraft or of components that could be expected from any given capacity, or the likely changes that would occur in Service demands either as a result of changes in their operations and the discovery of mistakes they had made, or as a result of the development of new designs. Yet in the process of co-ordination decisions had to be taken on assumptions, either expressly made or implied by default, about all these variables. The co-ordinators were essentially those who decided what risks should be taken and, of course, they were often wrong.

The problem of planning was also simplified by dealing with plans for a fixed point of time. In the jargon of economics individual plans were always thought of as being related to a single point of equilibrium, rather than as related to a set of continuously moving equilibria. Thus at any point of time MAP would be planning on the basis of an allocation of man-power which would relate to a point of time usually at most six months ahead. It would have no information about the man-power which would be available to it in successive periods after that point of time. For the interrelation between the employment of various departments at any particular point of time was a difficult enough problem for the central allocating authorities to comprehend; it was beyond their capacities to work out the varying relationship through time. As a consequence, MAP had to proceed on the assumption that it would be allowed to employ indefinitely the labour that it had been allocated for the current period, for MAP had to plan much of the capacity for aircraft production a few years rather than a few months ahead.

It is usually assumed, and quite wrongly, that planning decisions are timeless; or that if they take time, events can be made to stand still while the decisions are being taken. In fact, the time taken by the central planning authorities in reaching decisions about the conflicting claims of individual departments was substantial; for the resolution of such conflicts involved discussion, argument and counter-argument. It was not unusual, for example, for the discussion over man-power allocations to extend over a period of well over a month before decision was reached, by which time perhaps as much as two months of the six-monthly period under discussion had already passed. As the date for a central allocating committee review approached, the tempo of action in the departments slowed down, for there seemed to be little point in taking action which might have to be reversed when the decision of the allocating committee was taken. During the period of discussion and argument by the allocating committee the departments were filled with rumours as to the eventual outcome and the effect on their programmes; rumour and counter-rumour creating confusion, frustration and dismay throughout the department. And when the decision was taken there followed a period of frenzied activity when attempts were made to put into effect almost overnight the necessary changes in programmes, for this usually had to be done in great haste if the revised allocations were to be met.

The fact that planning decisions cannot be timeless also means that they must be discontinuous. For if any one decision takes time it is impossible for the central allocating authorities to take account of every change in the situation as it occurs. And the longer the intervals between the taking of decisions and the more important the changes actually taking place during the intervals, the bigger the upheaval that must take place at each planning stage. Hence arises the inescapable phenomenon of a planned system—that it must move in fits and starts. And not only must administrative decisions be discontinuous, but it must also take time for the latest decisions to seep through the system to the periphery where day to day action is taken.

It is perhaps an inevitable weakness of the human mind to conclude that the remedy for these glaring inefficiencies of the operation of economic planning in war-time was to improve the methods of planning and co-ordination, and to assume that there was some system which would work almost perfectly, if it could only be found. In my view this was and still remains the main fallacy of the planning theorist. For I would like to emphasize once again that all the difficulties which I have outlined arise from the limitations of human beings. To attempt to cure the inefficiencies of planning by even more planning, merely puts an even greater burden on the limited capacities of the administrators, and results, in the end, in the planning process becoming more, not less, inefficient. Indeed, planning and co-ordination was successful during the war only in so far as it was recognized that it had to be rough and ready; any attempt to operate a 'perfect' system would have made even limited co-ordination impossible. And yet it is one of the ironies of planning that the more ambitious the system of co-ordination constructed, the less likely was it to be successful; and the more limited and successful it was, the less useful its results. It followed from this that those who constructed theories of perfect planning were usually bad planners in practice, while those who were sceptical of the possibilities of over-all planning, usually operated successfully limited schemes of planning and co-ordination. Certainly the experience of MAP seems to demonstrate that the best planners are the anti-planners!

All these inevitable limitations in the planning process in war-time resulted in waste of resources. But this waste did not in general take the form of the unemployment of resources and it was, therefore, in the main not obvious to the public. In the case of MAP, for example, it led to the Services being provided with inferior aircraft, to aircraft being produced for which there was some vital component missing, or to excess components or spares being produced which merely accumulated in Service Department stores and were never used. In fact, so confused and inefficient did the whole process become at times, that the sceptics in MAP asserted, and there is little doubt that many of the firms agreed with them, that aircraft were produced in spite of, and not as a result of, MAP's planning activities.

It is important that we should realize that even the limited success of economic planning in war-time depended on the possession by Government Departments of the most powerful instruments for ensuring the execution of their plans. Of these I would rate as most important the fact that during the war a substantial part of the labour and resources of the country was employed either directly or indirectly on Government contracts. At the height of war mobilization, in June 1943, of a total employed population in Great Britain of over twenty-two million, five million were employed in the Defence Forces, and about five and a quarter million in manufacturing industries on orders for Supply Departments. In addition, many millions were employed in Government Service, Agriculture, Building, Mining and Distribution directly or indirectly on contracts for Government Departments. It was through the adjustment and alteration of these contracts that Government Departments were able to secure that their ever-changing plans were put into operation, and that the economic resources of the nation were distributed as the Government wished. Without the contract power the rearrangements and execution of plans would have been immeasurably more difficult, if not impossible. Take for example a decision by the labour allocating authorities that MAP was to get more labour and the Ministry of Supply less. This redistribution of the labour force would have been even more difficult than it was in fact, had not the Ministry of Supply cut its contracts to the extent which it thought necessary to release the required volume of labour, and MAP increased its contracts correspondingly. The direction of labour and the operation of differential wage payments were supplementary, and much inferior weapons, for securing the desired redistribution.

The importance of the power of contract action in securing the execution and co-ordination of plans can also be seen from the problems that MAP experienced in trying to secure the correct relationship between aircraft and component production. It was, for example, the fact that MAP itself placed the contracts for aero-engines and gave them out on 'embodiment loan' to the aircraft manufacturers to embody into the aircraft, that enabled it to determine what engines should be produced and who should get them when they had been produced. Where for special reasons, which I cannot go into here, it was considered inadvisable for MAP to place contracts—as for example in the case of undercarriages—its control over the uses to which production capacity was put was much more tenuous and remote. As a result it became an axiom of planning in MAP that there could be no programme without a contract, just as there should be no contract without a programme.

Secondly, vague and indeterminate though it was, there was a single criterion—the effective prosecution of the war— by which Government officials could judge the desirability of any action. And it was agreed that the responsibility for interpreting this criterion in terms of the strategy and tactics to be used had to be left to the Government and the Services.

Thirdly, in so far as inflationary tendencies were inevitable, they operated to a large extent to pull resources in the direction in which the Government desired. The rise in wages and prices took place most markedly in those sectors of the economy, especially in the munitions industries, where the Government wished to see labour and other resources transferred and they operated, therefore, to ease the process of changeover.

Lastly, most of the individuals in the community were agreed on the necessity of fighting the war, were prepared to regard the winning of the war as the primary objective of their lives as long as it lasted, and were prepared to leave to the Government and the Armed Forces the decisions as to how the war could best be fought. Apart from their willingness, or even anxiety, to accept restrictions on their freedom of choice both as consumers and producers, most of them realized the importance of refraining from taking action which would frustrate the decisions of the Government. It was fairly easy, for example, to persuade anyone employed in a munitions factory, whether he was an operative or a manager, that his actions might make the difference between life or death for someone in the Armed Forces, or success or failure in battle. He could also see the logic of the policy which demanded that he must accept the minimum standard of consumption for himself and his family which was necessary for the maintenance of their efficiency as productive units, and that he must surrender the rest of his income for the time being in taxation or saving.

It was the existence of these powerful instruments which made the direction of our economic resources, haphazard and inefficient though it sometimes was, at all possible.

I now want to discuss the relevance of my analysis of the reasons for war-time planning and the principal methods by which it was operated, to the problem of economic planning in peace-time. You will remember that I put forward four main reasons why planning was both necessary and desirable in war-time. They are the inevitability of inflationary tendencies in the economy which have to be kept in check by controls and rationing; the unwillingness and incompetence of the business men to take the risks involved in the production of weapons of war; the desire to feel that the economic process was subject to conscious control and that the course of events was not merely the result of blind chance; and, lastly, the over-riding necessity of using the resources of the nation to secure the single objective of winning the war in the way which the Government and the Armed Forces thought best.

It is to this last reason that I attach greatest importance as explaining both the desirability and necessity of detailed physical planning in war-time. I regard the three other reasons merely as particular cases of this general one. And I maintain that it is on this issue of whether there is a single objective in peace-time comparable to this war-time objective to provide not only the aim but also the criterion of correct policy, that the case for or against central economic planning in peace-time must depend.

Is there a single over-riding objective capable of clear and precise definition at which the community as a community is trying to aim in peace-time? Or are there in peace-time a multiplicity of objectives, arising largely from differences in the wishes of individuals, which cannot be reconciled in terms of a single objective? The planners hold the first view and quite logically say that planning is as essential in peace-time as in war, while the anti-planners take the second view and, as I think, quite logically say that there is no place in peace-time for the kind of planning that we had during the war, or in fact for any kind of central direction of the way in which the resources of the community should be used. It is this fundamental difference of view which explains the conflicting conclusions which two eminent temporary civil servants, Sir Oliver Franks and Professor Lionel Robbins, have drawn from their wide experience of economic planning in war-time.

Now it merely confuses the whole issue to say that in peace-time the 'National Interest' or the 'Good of all' takes the place of the war-time objective of defeating the enemy. For this merely raises the issue as to what is the 'National Interest'. Whether we are prepared to leave the decision as to what is in the National Interest to the Government and the planners, and whether even if this decision is left to them, it can be interpreted by them so as to provide a clear and consistent criterion of policy by which we can all be guided in our actions. Or whether we regard the National Interest as the development of the maximum amount of individual freedom, with each person being left to decide as far as possible what is best himself.

I feel that discussion of this issue is also confused by the quite separate question of the desirability of the State securing a redistribution of income between rich and poor. For the arguments for economic planning often put forward amount

F

to no more than the suggestion that control and rationing are necessary in order to secure 'fair shares for all'. This question ought to be treated quite separately from that of the desirability of planning in order to secure the fulfilment of some national purpose. The appropriate method of securing redistribution is through taxation, for the use of rationing and controls for this purpose not only restricts the field of individual choice and is, therefore, wasteful, but also means that the extent of redistribution is quite uncertain. The reply is often made that to secure the necessary redistribution through taxation in a free economy would involve such a high level of taxation that incentive would be very much blunted. I would suggest that there is no evidence for believing that redistribution through controls and rationing is any less harmful in this respect.

While it is quite clear that business men were both unwilling and incompetent to take the necessary risks in war-time, there is little evidence that this is so in peace-time, or that there is any other class in the community who would be better able to perform this function. For whatever evidence there is that in particular lines of activity the business man does not know what is in his best interests, that for example he refuses to introduce more up to date methods of manufacture even though these would be more profitable for him, it has never yet been shown that this is true of the generality of business men or that officials in Government Departments can be expected to be more enterprising.

As for inflation, while it was desirable in a mild form in the early years of the war, and, therefore, had to be controlled in order to keep it mild, there is little reason for believing that the inflation even of a mild character will help us in the changeover to peace. On the contrary it is now generally, although rather belatedly recognized, that the inflationary tendencies in our economy are frustrating and not helping the changeover to normal production, and that the remedy is not to dam up the inflation by planning and controls, but to take action to get rid of the inflation.

The argument that those in a favourable position should not be allowed to benefit by receiving windfall gains, applied equally to the changeover to peace-time production as it did to the initial changeover to war production. And, as I see it, this was the main case for retaining the whole apparatus of control in the initial post-war period. The period over which we regard physical control as necessary for this reason depends on how long we consider this transitional period lasts. There is indeed the possibility that physical controls will be used to drag the economy away from the shape that it would take in a free price system and, therefore, the period of abnormality will last indefinitely. This results in the argument that it is the existence of overall shortages that force controls and planning on us however much we may dislike them. But shortages are merely a sign of the lack of balance in our economy that physical planning and controls have failed to correct or have exaggerated. And so the argument feeds on itself. For the longer control is maintained, and the more those operating it try to work against the market forces, the greater will be the redistribution of resources that will have to take place once the controls are abolished. It is one thing to use controls in the transitional period in order to ease the changeover to a free system, and quite another to use them to frustrate the operation of such a system. If the latter is the main objective, then it means the indefinite continuation of controls, and the transitional period argument can no longer be given as the reason for retaining them.

There is no doubt that the passion for planning, which arises from a desire that the nation should consciously control its economic destiny, has assumed increasing importance in recent years and is probably just as important now as it was during the war. It is this desire which accounts, more than anything else, for the clamour which comes from practically every quarter for a grand plan for the whole economic activity of the nation which will show how the activity of each and every one of us fits into the general pattern. So far this clamour has remained unanswered, in my view because the production of such a grand plan is quite impossible and can indeed never be produced for the complex economic system in which we live. We have seen already that a master plan of this sort did not exist even in war-time. And whatever feeling of conscious control the process of planning gives to the planners it would indeed be a little difficult after the experience of the last two years to convince the planned that their destiny is being consciously controlled. Yet it is not sufficient to proclaim that this desire is merely a vain searching. It remains for those who feel that a free economy serves the purposes of the community better than a planned system, to educate the public into understanding that there is a certain rationale behind the working of the market mechanism, and that such a system does not operate exclusively through the blind forces of chance.

But, whatever your views may be about the theoretical desirability of central economic planning in peace-time, and however much the validity of the arguments that I have put forward may be questioned, it has to be recognized that the instruments for securing the execution of such plans in peace-time are immeasurably inferior to those that were available during the war. For suppose we are all prepared to agree that there is such a thing as 'the economic purpose of the nation', and that we are prepared to entrust to the Government the decision as to what this purpose is, how does the Government proceed to work out a co-ordinated and consistent plan in all its detail and secure its execution? First of all, it is clear that the drawing up of such a plan must be left to someone with enormous power. Perhaps you will allow me to quote from Sir Oliver Franks who expresses this view so clearly in his lectures on 'Central Economic Planning in War and Peace'. He says: 'it follows then that the attainment of that unity of purpose which is required by central planning and control makes a heavy call on leadership. There must be leadership within the Government. The framing of the idea, the general plan of management for the National economy, requires a leader to resolve the difficult but legitimate differences that may be expected to exist within the Government about the way in which the balance of resources should be struck.' But the leader would need to have, not only the immense power which Sir Oliver Franks' statement implies, but also infinite wisdom and time to ensure that the balance which he strikes is really a balance, that his decisions about the use of resources for one purpose are consistent with all his other decisions. And unless he can work out the whole detailed plan himself in his infinite wisdom, he must of necessity delegate to others the interpretation and execution in detail of his general instructions. With what criteria can he provide his officials to ensure that the various ways in which they interpret his general directions are consistent with one another? Unless he can do this, one set of officials may be allocating new investment in one way while another set are directing labour in ways which are quite inconsistent.

You will remember that I laid great emphasis on Departmental programmes in war-time as the main instrument through which the decisions of different allocating authorities were linked together, and that I considered these Departmental programmes effective because they represented contracts. This contract power of the Government is much more restricted in peace-time, at least at present. If we are really to attempt planning even on the restricted scale on which it was operated in war-time, then the direct contract power of the Government will have to be extended. It will, for example, be quite impossible to have an export programme in any way comparable in function and effectiveness to the aircraft programme that we had during the war, unless the Government is prepared to back its export targets with contracts just as the aircraft programme was backed in war-time. The suggestion that the function performed by contract action can be fulfilled equally well by control of the allocation of materials is an illusion which is likely to have disastrous consequences if acted upon. There are those who would welcome the extension of Government contract action to cover the whole field of the economy. If such a system were attempted the variety of products that would have to be dealt with would be immeasurably greater than during the war, and the problem of co-ordinating all the different sets of contracts in order to secure their consistency with each other would be infinitely more complex and unmanageable.

I have neglected to deal with the problems of wage policy and incentives under a centrally planned economy, not because I feel they are unimportant but because I want to emphasize that even if the Government were given the most drastic powers, the sheer administrative problem of working out a detailed consistent plan for the economic activities of an industrial system as large and as complex as ours is quite unmanageable.

You will no doubt have concluded by this time that I do not regard central economic planning in the sense which it is usually understood as either workable or appropriate to our peace-time economic system. Before I sit down I would like to make it quite clear that I do not wish it to be assumed that I am in favour of 'unbridled free enterprise' uncontrolled by the State. It is in fact my view that there are many extremely important spheres where the State alone can secure the efficient working of the economic system, for example in the control of monopoly and in securing full employment. I am merely concerned to try and show that such action should be taken within the framework of a market system. But to demonstrate that action which is appropriate to the Government can in fact be successfully taken within the framework of a free price system, would take me many more hours and since I have already tried your patience overmuch, I will desist.

5

Treasury Control

I

THERE are many pitfalls in basing conclusions on evidence given before the Select Committee on Estimates. But Treasury officials appear so rarely in public to explain their activities, that it is difficult to resist the temptation to make use of the evidence given to the Select Committee in its examination of Treasury Control of Expenditure. It is not possible to comment within the space of a single paper on the whole range of evidence presented to the Committee. Apart from many interesting Memoranda put in by the Treasury and the Departments, oral evidence, extending to 3,121 questions and answers, was given by senior civil servants, and important ex-civil servants. To deal with the whole of this, and the Report of the Committee on it all, one would have to write quite a long book. I pick out some of the major issues which interest me particularly and which deserve to be widely discussed.[3]

Treasury Control can be considered under four main headings. First, as part of the traditional, constitutional and Parliamentary system for controlling finance; second, as part of the function of the Chancellor of the Exchequer in budgetary policy, both in the narrower fiscal context of balancing expenditure and taxation and borrowing, and in the wider context of general economic policy; third, as an instrument for securing economy and preventing waste in the detailed expenditure of Departments; and fourth, as an instrument for securing efficiency in the use of resources by the Government in relation to the broad objects of policy. I am not here

---

[1] A paper read to the Staff Seminar in Economics at Manchester University, February 1959.

[2] Sixth Report from the Select Committee on Estimates, Session 1957–8: Treasury Control of Expenditure (HMSO, 1958).

[3] And one hopes are being considered by Lord Plowden who is undertaking an enquiry for the Government into the whole system of Treasury control.

concerned with the first of these, but will take the other three and comment on the light thrown on them by the evidence given by Treasury officials and civil servants from other departments to the Committee.

II

One of the main uses of the system of Annual Estimates and the rule that no new service may be introduced without Treasury approval, is to ensure that the total expenditure of Government Departments, both actual and prospective, is kept within bounds. The general picture that emerges from the evidence, is that in terms of influence on Departments these two instruments are the most important aspects of Treasury control. The most effective argument that the Treasury can use to a Department wishing to spend more either on existing services or on new items is, 'we are terribly sorry, but there just is not the money'. Both Treasury witnesses and those from the spending Departments emphasized that this control over the *amount* of expenditure was the major influence which the Treasury exercised over Departments. Sir Norman Brook (Joint Permanent Secretary to the Treasury) stated, 'of course, good value is very important, but the Chancellor has to provide from the taxpayer for all this expenditure. He must inevitably be concerned with the amount of it as with the question whether it is well spent, and Treasury control is directed primarily to the amount of it.' (3015.)[1] There is general corroboration of this view by the Permanent Secretaries of the main spending Departments.

One of the main problems that the Treasury faces in keeping overall expenditure under control, is that it is difficult to foresee at the time of its first introduction what any new item or service is eventually going to cost, and that, in some services, rising expenditure is determined by factors which are very often outside the control of Departments.[2] This difficulty is increased by the system of annual Estimates which focuses attention on expenditure within the next twelve months and pays little, if any attention, to the commitment for later years implicit in that expenditure. One of the most interesting features of the Treasury evidence is the disclosure

[1] All references in (   ) are to question numbers in the Report.
[2] E.g. rising expenditure on education with increased numbers of children staying on at school after 15.

that a system of financial programmes looking ahead for three years is being used for some major fields of expenditure, such as defence, hospitals and roads. Indeed, in their observations on the recommendations of the Select Committee, the Treasury state 'forecasts of all civil expenditure, up to three years ahead, have been prepared annually for many years past'.[1] This was not made clear in the main evidence of the Committee, and there is, therefore, no information in the evidence explaining the nature and use of these three-year estimates for civil expenditure.[2] This extension of financial planning three years, rather than one year, ahead, is, of course, of the greatest importance. Public debate and argument about Government expenditure would be much more useful and to the point, if these three-year programmes were made available to the House of Commons and debated there. At present they are given only occasionally for particular items of expenditure.

In exercising this function of keeping expenditure down, the Treasury are primarily concerned with total expenditure, and when a cut has to be made either in the estimates or in actual expenditure, the Treasury tend to confine themselves to securing an overall cut of the right size. They apparently pay little attention to where the cut should fall within each Department's expenditure. This tends to encourage a system of rather arbitrary percentage cuts all round.

There is little evidence that in controlling expenditure, the Treasury relate finance to other resources, and take these into account in deciding which to prune and where to allow expansion. This is done occasionally, as for example, in relating defence expenditure to the use of technical and scientific man-power, but this seems to be an exception.[3]

---

[1] Seventh Special Report from the Select Committee on Estimates, Session 1958–9. Treasury Control of Expenditure (observations of the Treasury), (HMSO, 1959).

[2] See (2256)—(2258) for a discussion of the development of three-year programmes for Defence Expenditure.

[3] Sir Richard Powell, Permanent Secretary and Accounting Officer, Ministry of Defence, 'As I said, the criticism is primarily directed to the total size of the programme and its financial manageability, with, maybe, certain special questions, such as whether we were planning to absorb a higher proportion of scientific and technical manpower for Research and Development than they thought was reasonable in the economic situation of the country—that broad kind of question.'

III

On the Treasury's function of securing economy and checking waste in Departmental expenditure, there are two main
issues. First, how far, and in what detail, should the Treasury
intervene in Departmental affairs; and second, what instruments should the Treasury use in controlling and checking
Departmental waste and potential inefficiency.

There are two principles tugging in opposite directions.
First, that nothing should be done to impair Departmental
responsibility. This would reduce Treasury intervention to a
minimum, since if the Treasury intervened in detail, the
Department could escape responsibility by claiming that it
was merely acting in accordance with Treasury instructions.
At the other extreme is the principle that the Treasury has
responsibility, as the public's watchdog, for making sure that
not one penny of the taxpayer's money is wasted, and the
efficient carrying out of this responsibility would require
frequent and detailed scrutiny of Departmental expenditure.
In practice these two extremes would be represented, on the
one hand, by the view that once the Estimates were made
Departments should be allowed to spend up to the total of
these estimates without sanction on detail, even on new
items of expenditure, from the Treasury; on the other hand,
by the view that every item of expenditure, however small,
should be subject to Treasury sanction. In fact no witness
argued in favour of either extreme, but a great deal of the
discussion at the Committee was on the question whether in
practice the right balance between the two was being achieved.

It could, of course, be argued, that if the Departments were
being run properly, intervention by the Treasury on matters
of detail in order to secure economy, should be quite unnecessary. After all the Departments themselves have their
own finance divisions, and the financial responsibility of the
Departments is recognized administratively by having the
Permanent Secretary also as Accounting Officer. On this view
the Treasury should regard as its most important function,
seeing to it that each Department has the proper internal
arrangements and administrative structure to secure control
and economy of expenditure and the prevention of waste.
If Departmental arrangements were efficient, the need for
external detailed control by the Treasury would be reduced.

The case for this method of securing efficiency was put frequently by members of the Committee.

In fact it is Treasury practice to review Departmental organization with this in mind and some examples of such reviews are given in the Treasury's evidence.[1] These reviews are however, *ad hoc*, and there is no general programme for reviewing each Department in turn every so often. It is also clear from the evidence that while the Treasury attach importance to such reviews, they do not regard them as the main instrument for securing economy and efficiency or as adequate substitutes for direct Treasury supervision and control of Departmental expenditure.

The Treasury recognize, of course, that detailed control over every item of expenditure, is neither possible nor desirable, and there is in existence a system of delegation of authority to the Departments for certain items of expenditure. The existing system of delegated authority can only be explained as an historical development, with the position being reviewed on an *ad hoc* basis in response to pressure from particular departments. Many apparently ludicrous cases, where Treasury authority has to be obtained in advance, still remain. And the Treasury view that it is quite right that Departments should not be allowed to overspend even to a small extent, albeit on essential items, dies hard. The Committee spent a great deal of time on this issue of delegation, cross-examining each Department in turn on it as well as the Treasury witnesses. I quote below, the cross-examination of the Treasury on one example—the limitation of delegated authority to the Ministry of Defence for expenditure on maps to £2,000 a year—because it illustrates very well the issues involved and the Treasury attitude to them.

Mr Robinson[2]
(2948). The point I am trying to make is, could not the Treasury allow the Ministry of Defence to spend on maps what they thought was fit in the course of a year?—(Sir Thomas Padmore[3]). Again, it would not be a terrible matter if open-ended delegated authority were given, but as things

[1] Select Committee Report, Appendix 7, pp. 393-4.
[2] A member of the Committee.
[3] A Second Secretary, the Treasury.

go, as a general rule, when a proposition is made for delegated authority of this sort, one fixes the level at a figure which will cover anything reasonable, and the only virtue of the £2,000 limit in that case is that the Treasury should at any rate come to know about it if, for some reason, which is not very likely, the Ministry of Defence goes rather wild. But I cannot pretend that it is a matter of any great importance.

Chairman[1]
(2949). This boils down to the fact that on the face of it there are ridiculous limitations, not ridiculous but curious limitations, which must detract from the sense of responsibility of the department involved. After all, it is the office of the Treasury to build up a sense of responsibility in the Departments. This attitude, 'we will give you this far and no further', detracts from the sense of responsibility of a Department, does it not?—It would if these were, as they are usually not in the case of these small delegations, really limiting delegations. What happens is that the Department says, 'we want to do so and so' and we ask, 'How much do you want?'. If they say, 'Something inside £2,000', we say 'All right, £2,000', and we do not hear any more about it.

Mr Robinson
(2950). But somebody in the Department must keep a close eye on expenditure of maps in the course of a year, because he will get into serious trouble if he spends £2,100 and does not inform the Treasury?—(Sir Norman Brook[2]). Is that necessarily a bad thing?
(2951). I would think that it was?—I can imagine a Ministry of Defence—I do not say the present Ministry—going quite mad over maps and plunging in with great quantities of expensive types of maps. I do not think it unreasonable that there should be some limit.

Chairman
(2952). Surely this brings up the fundamental principle, do you or do you not expect your Departments and Heads of Departments to be men of a sense of responsibility and ability? Surely the principle should be to give them freedom

[1] Sir Godfrey Nicholson.
[2] Joint Permanent Secretary to the Treasury and Secretary of the Cabinet.

and to chase them like hell if they abuse it, rather than this sort of governess attitude of letting them out on a lead?— I am sorry, but I think that the primary object of these delegations is to avoid a lot of unnecessary applications to the Treasury and unnecessary correspondence about small things, and that the figures were fixed in relation to each subject at a level which would obviate that kind of correspondence.

(2953). And against the Head of a Department showing any sense of responsibility?—(Sir Thomas Padmore). Only very partially, because in this case, the maps for instance, Sir Richard Powell[1] said that some of these delegations and some of these requirements for references to the Treasury were helpful to him as accounting officer, because so many of the small things in the machine of a great Department are dealt with a fairly long way down the line. As a practical matter, there is some advantage in the man down the line, who deals with small matters in the Ministry of Defence, having some check plus that imposed on him by his own accounting officer. The extent to which an accounting officer in a Department like the Ministry of Defence can occupy himself with expenditure on maps is very limited.

(2954). You are getting yourself into a most dangerous position. You are saying that the function of the Treasury is not only to be the long-stop, but to do the function of the accounting officer?—With respect, I am not saying that. I am saying that there is a good deal to be said for having a check on the man buying maps for the Ministry of Defence.

(2959). That is the function of the accounting officer of the Ministry of Defence, is it not?—So it is, but there is certainly an advantage in some of the delegation limits in that the check is automatically and easily provided by the necessity, if the expenditure goes beyond what has been previously agreed to be a reasonable level, for a report to be made to the Treasury.

(2956). I am very sorry, but I think you are advancing a very dangerous doctrine. You are saying that a Department of that kind cannot be trusted to do its own work, or is not capable of doing its own work, and the Treasury must be in the background to stop the balls which go by the wicket

[1] Permanent Secretary and Accounting Officer, Ministry of Defence, who had given evidence to the Committee earlier.

keeper in order to stop the byes?—That is not what I intended to say.

There are many other cases of this kind on which the Departments and the Treasury are cross-examined. Clearly the Committee was worried, and they are not alone in this, by the striking contrast between the time spent by the Treasury on the minutae of Departmental expenditure, and the apparent ease with which estimates for major items of expenditure could be exceeded, for example in research and development, with the Treasury very often ignorant of what had been happening until the damage was done.

IV

How can the Treasury tell, when it looks at Departmental estimates, or when the Department submits a request for new expenditure, whether the Department is being as efficient and economical as possible? It is part of the general theory of Treasury control, which fits in with the theory of the general operation of the British civil service, that Treasury officials are not experts on any particular aspects, financial or other, of Departmental operations. The criticism they apply is, therefore, based on the kind of question which an 'intelligent layman' might ask. The 'intelligent layman' theory of Treasury examination of Department expenditure, runs throughout the evidence given to the Committee. 'The business of Treasury control is, in essence, the exercise by laymen of judgment upon the proposals of experts. It is no part of the Treasury business to attempt to rival the Departments in the expert knowledge which they possess in their own field. What is necessary is to test the projects put forward and to obtain enough information to form a judgment as to whether the schemes are well founded; to make sure that enthusiasm does not run ahead of prudence and common-sense . . . '.[1] Sir John Woods[2] took the same view saying, 'A very distinguished Treasury official of my time, Sir Gilbert Upcott, who was afterwards Comptroller and Auditor-General, once defined the job of the Treasury in relation to

[1] Memorandum submitted by the Treasury, Select Committee Report p. 4.
[2] Permanent Secretary of the Board of Trade when he left the public service in 1951.

the control of expenditure as being that of a first-class common law barrister cross-examining an expert witness, and that view I have always personally accepted as being right.' (1622). Again when a member of the Committee suggested that the Treasury might use cost accountants to watch the efficient execution of Government contracts, the reply came, 'Not in the Treasury. The function of the Treasury is that of a lay critic.' (147).

It is also argued that knowledge that Treasury criticism has to be met, itself exercises a salutary discipline on Departments, and induces them to think about their policies and practices in ways which might not otherwise occur to them. This view is put most effectively by Sir Frank Lee.[1] 'Supposing we were suggesting a revised and expanded scheme of financial assistance to the film production industry. That would have to be worked up by one of my people in the form of a memorandum, which would set out the policy objectives, the reasons for these, the financial implications, and so on, and I certainly hope that that memorandum would itself be a pretty complete and critical, almost ice-cold, appraisement of the proposals. Nevertheless, I do think the necessity of carrying that one stage further and talking to the Treasury about it may well give rise to some useful second thoughts. For our sins we live with these problems, of the cinema industry, and there is a tendency not to see the wood for the trees, and to write out a submission to the Treasury is a good discipline.' (2559).

Some Departmental witnesses argued that it is necessary for Treasury officials to be concerned with the detail of Departmental expenditure, so that they could be educated in Departmental problems, and so have the knowledge needed to exercise sympathetically the 'intelligent layman critic' function on important issues of expenditure. This view was put by Sir Frederick Hoyer Millar.[2] 'I should say that the value of consulting the Treasury at that stage is, perhaps, from our point of view—one does not want to put it rudely—an educative one: in other words, keeping the Treasury informed of how things are going on and how foreign policy

[1] Permanent Secretary, Board of Trade.
[2] Permanent Under-Secretary of State and Accounting Officer, the Foreign Office.

works, how the projects are working out, and the sort of things we have to do. That does help the Treasury to exercise their function as lay critic intelligently. It is difficult for us, unless they have some knowledge of the current operations.' (1526).

V

How effective is this lay criticism? Does the Treasury ever make suggestions and comments which have been overlooked by Departments? Is it, in any case, adequate as a means of securing economy and value for money on the broad distribution, as well as on the minutae, of expenditure? The view is frequently expressed by the Departments that apart from control over the total amount of expenditure,[1] the influence of the Treasury is negligible. I give below a sample of Departmental replies on this important point.

Ministry of Supply
(1996). Chairman: Are programmes sometimes modified in timing and phrasing as a result of Treasury criticism?—(Mr Dunnett[2]). I cannot think of any case in which it has been modified because of Treasury criticism, but in the case of a large store like a V-bomber they are extremely interested in the rate of production from the broad financial point of view, and they might take it even to ministerial level and say that the country cannot afford that rate per annum of production of a really big store like an aircraft.
(1997). Only as keepers of the purse and not as helpful lay critics?—I would agree with what Sir Cyril[3] has said, that on the details of the programme the Treasury rarely make a point that we have not thought of.

Ministry of Health
(1254) Mr Robinson.[4] To what extent does the Treasury investigation of these schemes[5] have the effect of modifying the scheme . . . ?(Mr Gedling[6]). The answer to that is that the

[1] Which is dealt with in Section II of this article.
[2] A Deputy Secretary, Ministry of Supply.
[3] Sir Cyril Musgrave, Permanent Secretary and Accounting Officer, Ministry of Supply.
[4] A member of the Committee.
[5] For Hospitals.
[6] An Assistant Secretary, Hospitals and Specialist Services Division, the Ministry of Health.

amount of change nowadays by Treasury examination is very
small indeed . . .

(1255). Vice-Admiral Hughes Hallett[1]—Does the Treasury
ever draw your attention to improved methods—some more
economical form of heating system, for example, which they
might have found out through their contacts with the
Ministry of Works, shall we say?—(Sir John Hawton[2]) I
should have thought generally not.

Foreign Office
(1525). Chairman—I was asking whether the criticisms on
the project, by and large, are valuable?—(Sir Dennis Allen[3])
From the point of view of saving money, I should have thought
that the effect was very small. The cases in which the
Treasury suggestions or criticisms really make much
difference in the long run to the amount spent are pretty rare.

Admiralty
(2696). Vice-Admiral Hughes Hallett—I was going to ask
whether your officers felt they themselves have benefited in
any marked degree by the counsel and advice of the Treasury
officials?—(Sir Victor Shepheard[4]) Yes, they came back very
pleased and they told me that they felt it was a good thing
they went because the Treasury had not got a right impression but, when they asked questions, they understood what
the project was about and the benefit we would get from it.

(2697). Mr Robinson—Did they feel the operation was
necessary or useful from your point of view? No doubt it was
educative to the Treasury, but was it from your point of
view?—I would say yes, definitely. Otherwise, we might
have lost the project.

(2698). Vice-Admiral Hughes Hallett—May I interpose a
question? The value from your point of view was that you
got the money? You would be prepared to have the money
without Treasury control—Oh! yes.

In considering the Treasury method of control as the
'intelligent layman' cross-examining 'experts' from the
Departments, it is important to realize that the officials of
Departments who deal with the Treasury are expert only in

---

[1] A member of the Committee.
[2] Permanent Secretary and Accounting Officer, the Ministry of Health.
[3] Deputy Under-Secretary of State (Chief Clerk), the Foreign Office.
[4] Director of Naval Construction.

a comparative sense. For the officials from the Departments are normally from the administrative class. The Treasury has little contact with the technical staff of the Departments.

(38). Vice-Admiral Hughes Hallett. When you used the term Administrative Officer of the Ministry of Supply,[1] would you include the Directors-General of the various Departments, such as the Director-General of Air Material, or in the Service Departments would it include a general or an air marshal?—(Mr MacPherson[2]) Not normally, no. It would be through the administrative officer, someone in the administrative grade who might bring with him a Service officer dealing with this particular project. We would not have direct contact with the serving officers.
(2142). When the Treasury intervene and you have to go, shall we say, to a meeting at the Treasury on whether some project should be continued or modified, would your finance officers normally take the technical advisers with them to such a meeting?—(Sir Cyril Musgrave[3]) I think normally no; but there would be many exceptions to that.

Within each Department itself, of course, the administrative class official also acts as the 'intelligent lay critic' of the expert technical divisions, and the criticism and comment by the Treasury is, therefore, normally of one set of intelligent lay critics by another. Is this double banking of lay critics either useful or necessary? On this point Sir Cyril Musgrave[3] said, 'May I say that if a case turns up, such as the one I have just mentioned, where the Treasury, being layman, raise points that should in my judgment have been raised by my own lay financial critics, I would want to know why they were not raised before they went to the Treasury, and so would my deputy secretaries and under-secretaries; and if one finds a case like that, the finance officer who is letting the thing go to the Treasury without asking questions which obviously a layman can pose has got to answer for his failure.' (2184)
The Treasury official, although a lay critic, does in practice, it is argued, pick up a great deal of expertese by specializing

[1] As indicating the normal channel of liaison with the Treasury.
[2] An Assistant Secretary and a Treasury Officer of Accounts, the Treasury.
[3] Permanent Secretary and Accounting Officer, Ministry of Supply.

for a time on a particular Department or group of Departments. In addition, there will always be in the Treasury officials who have experience of work in the Departments, and vice versa, since in principle interchange of staff between the Departments and the Treasury is encouraged as a matter of policy. On the first point the evidence given by the Treasury suggests that, in fact, staff hardly spend sufficient time in any particular division to acquire and make use of specialist knowledge. Thus of 106 principals and assistant secretaries in the Treasury in January 1958, forty-one had been in their existing division less than one year, and thirty-eight between one and two years. Only fourteen out of 106 had more than three years in their existing division.[1] The evidence on the second point appears to give greater support to the argument. Of the 106 principals and assistant secretaries, seventy-four had some service with other Departments.[2] But these figures relate to the Treasury as a whole, and one cannot tell whether they apply equally well to the divisions dealing with supply expenditure. It certainly does not seem to operate in the case of the Ministry of Supply.

(2192). Chairman—Is there much interchange of officers between you and the Treasury?—(Sir Cyril Musgrave[3]) No, not between ourselves and the Treasury; there is practically none, unfortunately, and I regret that very much.

(2193). Has it got worse?—I do not think it could get worse; there has hardly been any. I have one deputy secretary who came to me from the Treasury, and I can think of one principal who went from us to the Treasury, but she is on the establishment side.

VI

The Committee spent a great deal of time directed towards discovering whether the 'intelligent layman' principle is adequate for controlling the vast range of Government expenditure, not merely to check waste in detail, but also in the much wider context of securing value for money in relation to the broad objectives of policy. In some branches

[1] See Committee Report, Appendix 1, Table C, pp. 382.
[2] Op. cit., Table B, pp. 381.
[3] Permanent Secretary and Accounting Officer, Ministry of Supply.

of expenditure the Treasury, in fact, exercise control in method and extent which implies expert, rather than layman's knowledge on their part. The outstanding case is the control of establishments. Here the Treasury consider themselves in most matters as experts, at least as expert as the Departments. They exercise a very detailed control over manpower used by the Departments, have their own organization and methods division which advises Departments, and have inspectors visiting the Departments. Indeed some would argue that the establishments divisions in the Departments themselves are really outposts of the Treasury. The Committee asked whether the system of inspectors used in the control of establishments could not also be applied on the supply side. The reply was:

'The problems are really very different. In supply work, which is of enormous variety, there is not anything which corresponds to the standards of grading, the standards of staffing, the standards of organization and methods, account procedure, and so on, which on the establishment side can be applied as common standards to Departments however various: there is not the same generality of problems on the supply side which is amenable to inspection to ensure common standards everywhere.' (273).

Without going into the matter in detail, I would suggest that this exaggerates the real difference. One wonders how far the concentration of Treasury control on establishments is a matter of history, a relic of the time when to control Government Department establishment was the most effective means of controlling Government expenditure.

Another field of expenditure in which the Treasury go beyond that of lay critic, is in expenditure on food and agricultural subsidies. It is clear from the Treasury evidence and that of the Ministry of Agriculture, that Treasury officials play a substantial role in the annual review of farm prices, and that in this role, the expert knowledge they have from the Economic Section and the Overseas Finance Division of the Treasury, on the economic implications of agricultural policy and the relative cost of home output and imports, plays an important part. Certainly without this expertese behind them, the comment and criticism of Treasury officials would have much less substance.

The question whether the Treasury has sufficient expertese to watch and examine some of the broader issues of efficient expenditure is one of the important issues which emerges from this evidence. For while much of the questioning, especially on delegation, was directed to suggesting that Treasury control of the minutae of expenditure was unnecessary, members of the Committee came back time and time again to the need for analyses of expenditure and enquiries into efficiency in much broader terms. Important examples are the analysis of experience in planning and forward estimating research and development programmes, examination of prices and profits on Defence contracts, the study of the comparative efficiency of firms doing Government work, the development of standards in providing hospital facilities, and a comparative study of the cost of building work undertaken by different Departments.[1] These, and other suggestions, would imply an organized continuing study by experts of important aspects of Government expenditure, rather than *ad hoc* criticism by laymen of the Estimates and proposed expenditure.

One could indeed argue that there is scope for even more penetrating analysis in practically every major item of Government expenditure. In social service expenditure, for example, practically nothing is done either by the Treasury or the Departments to discover who in fact benefits from this expenditure, and without this it is difficult to discuss whether the present pattern and scale of expenditure meets the supposed objectives of Government policy. Enquiries of this kind, as well as those implied in the questions put by the Committee, could only be effectively undertaken by operational research divisions, either in the Treasury or the Departments, with technically qualified and experienced staff. Such divisions are apparently a regular feature of Government Departments in the United States.

The development of such divisions in British Government Departments would, of course, mean a considerable departure from the traditional view that efficiency and economy in Government expenditure, in both the broad and narrow aspects, can be achieved by the administrative grade staff

---

[1] Evidence given to the Committee suggested that studies of the last two of these were in fact being undertaken.

as intelligent lay critics. It would also mean an expansion of
the staff in the Treasury responsible for controlling and
examining supply expenditure. It is not generally realized
how tiny is the group of officials at the Treasury who bear
this enormous burden. In January 1958, the total administrative and executive staff in the Treasury, in divisions
concerned with the control of expenditure, was 275. Of this
195 were concerned with establishment and O.M., and
only forty-three with supply expenditure.[1] Expenditure on
the social services,[2] food and agriculture, and defence
material,[3] was looked after by two under-secretaries, four
assistant secretaries, twelve principals, four assistant principals, and thirteen executive officers.[4] Is it any wonder that one
witness said to the Committee, 'I do not know whether you
can visualize what the Treasury is like in December and
January,[5] but it is absolutely chaotic'. (2420).

[1] The remaining 37 were in 'mixed divisions' concerned with both establishments and expenditure.

[2] Education, Labour, Health, Housing, Local Government, Pensions and
National Insurance.

[3] The Defence Programme.

[4] Committee Report, Appendix 1, Table A, pp. 381.

[5] When the Estimates are being prepared.

PART II

Economic Statistics

6

The Language of Economic Statistics[1]

LET me explain at the outset that I am not going to discuss esoteric or abstract aspects of statistical theory. I have no claim whatsoever to be in any way expert in statistical theory or in the highly fashionable field of econometrics. I have never drawn up a linear programme or inverted a matrix; I am a stranger to model building; and I cannot oscillate a time series or properly analyse a variance. My acquaintance with economic statistics is much more mundane. If I have any title to be at all expert in statistics, and my title is a very tenuous one, it is in the use of economic statistics to describe the main features of our economic system and to portray its changing pattern through time.

In the last century, and with ever accelerating speed, in the last twenty or thirty years, there has been a great increase in the desire to measure and describe events quantitatively and as a consequence to collect and use more and more statistical information. Every economic and social situation or problem is now described in statistical terms, and we feel that it is such statistics which give us the real basis of fact for understanding and analysing problems and difficulties, and for suggesting remedies. In the main we use such statistics or figures without any elaborate theoretical analysis; little beyond totals, simple averages and perhaps index numbers. Figures have become the language in which we describe our economy or particular parts of it, and the language in which we argue about policy.

In this paper I want to discuss some of the important characteristics of statistics used as a language in this way. As will soon be realized, my remarks are mainly directed to pointing out the limitations of the statistical approach and the great difficulties and pitfalls in using the language. I am not going to point out the great advantages of being able to

[1] The first of four Newmarch Lectures given at University College, London, February 1954.

discuss and analyse situations in statistical terms. We have become so impressed with statistics, that I think such advantages are not likely to be overlooked. But in confining my attention mainly to limitations and difficulties in using statistics, I do not wish my view to be misinterpreted and it be thought that I hold that the use of statistics is always dangerous and misleading, although I suspect, notwithstanding this declaimer on my part, it will be thought that I am not far from putting forward such a radically destructive point of view.

The two most important characteristics of the language of statistics are first, that it describes things in quantitative terms, and second, that it gives this description an air of accuracy and precision. The limitations, as well as the advantages, of the statistical approach arise from these two characteristics. For a description of the quantitative aspect of events never gives us the whole story; and even the best statistics are never, and never can be, completely accurate and precise. To avoid misuse of the language we must, therefore, guard against exaggerating the importance of the elements in any situation that can be described quantitatively, and we must know sufficient about the error and inaccuracy of the figures to be able to use them with discretion.

There are those who are so impressed by the notion that 'quantification' is the only form of scientific knowledge, that they see no danger in the distorted, misleading, or simply ineffective picture that a statistical description of events may give. To such people the statistical picture is always to be preferred as the most meaningful and objective. It is indeed because this view is so widespread, that an argument stated in statistical terms has such a powerful influence in policy discussion, and induces everyone to try to impress their case on public attention by peppering it with statistics.

From such a viewpoint even the experience of falling in love could be adequately described in terms of statistics. A record of heart beats per minute, the stammering and hesitation in speech, the number of sighs per hour, the falling off in appetite, measured by the number of calories consumed per day, the heightening of poetic vision, measured by the number of lines of poetry written to the beloved—I won't go on; no doubt you can think of further measures. But I wonder

how many of those who have been through this experience
would feel that such statistics, however numerous and
elaborate, would in any significant sense describe the experience. It might provide an amusing satirical article for *Punch*,
but the essential emotional aspect of the experience would be
missing. Here most of us would recognize the inefficiency of
the statistical language compared with the language of
poetry, music, painting or the novel.

But once we leave extreme cases of this kind it is amazing
how frequently people grasp at statistics as the most powerful
medium of expression.

Let me illustrate by giving a real example. One of the most
perplexing features of road accidents is the way in which the
heavy toll of life which occurs day by day is treated by the
public with a shrug of the shoulders. A group of official
research workers, concerned to change this attitude, and
convinced that greater expenditure on various accident prevention measures, including improving the roads, would
result in a substantial reduction in accidents, came to the
conclusion that the most convincing way of judging the
'profitability' of various measures of expenditure on accident
prevention was to measure statistically the loss that the
nation suffered through road casualties. The damage to
vehicles and property, the medical costs, and the administrative costs of insurance, are in principle all measurable in
money terms. The loss due to deaths is not so easy. But,
nothing daunted, these research workers proceeded on the
basis that the loss due to a death of a person is equal, 'gross',
to the expected production of that person during the remainder of his life had he not been killed, using average expec-
tation of life figures; and the 'net loss', the difference between
this and his expected 'consumption'. On this basis the 'value'
of an individual to the community, is the difference between
his expected production and expected consumption.

This seems to me to be a case of 'quantification' gone mad.
Apart from the very substantial margin of error in the
statistics used in such a calculation, the whole idea seems to
me misguided, if not ludicrous. Estimating the 'net loss' to
the community in this way leads, for example, to the fantastic
result that if only we could have more road accidents in which
we succeeded in knocking down and killing old people we

should reduce the 'net loss'. For every death here is a net gain, since their expected production is zero and consumption positive. Indeed if we could only kill off enough old people we could show a net gain on accidents as a whole!

It is not merely the particular calculation which is open to criticism, but the mistaken emphasis that such calculations give to the measurable and economic aspects of road accidents. Surely these pale into insignificance compared with the suffering, misery and tragedy which result every day from such accidents. It is indeed a sad commentary on the state of the public conscience if we have to be persuaded that measures to reduce road accidents will pay, in some economic sense, before we will listen seriously.

My second example arose out of a desire to arrive at a rational, scientific basis for measuring the worthwhileness of social service expenditure and assessing how it should be distributed. The calculations were merely suggestions made at a discussion I attended. I do not think that in fact the research has been carried out. One method suggested was to compare statistically the cost of the service with the value of the benefits; to compare for example the costs and benefits of the national health service. But there is no objective way of doing this except by measuring both cost and benefit in terms of expenditure, thus demonstrating that the health service is worth just what is spent on it! The alternative was then put forward of measuring benefits in terms of the reduced incidence of sickness, such reduction to be valued in terms of the increase in the 'national product' as a result of fewer days away from work. Would this really tell us anything about the 'value' of the health service? Is there really any sense in judging the value of health by the criterion of the increase in the national income that it makes possible?

These are possibly exaggerated examples of the misuse of the language of economic statistics. But in many commoner uses of economic statistics, when for example we compare national income per head in this country now with a hundred years ago, and now in this country with the United States or India, we always run the risk of exaggerating the importance of the measurable. It is, of course, not easy to draw up any general principles which will tell us in what circumstances the language of statistics is likely to be misleading or inappropriate. We have each to use our judgment. I myself have always felt, for example, that the film I saw on the conditions in Belsen gave me a better, more vivid, and more real description of life in a concentration camp in Germany than innumerable tables of statistics could do. Indeed where the imaginative reconstruction of some entirely different situation with which we are not familiar is involved, I always find the language of statistics an unsatisfactory means of communication and description. For most purposes the statistical and non-statistical should be complementary, not opposing, means of communication, but we must beware of treating the statistical always as the more important, merely because we think of it as scientific and objective.

Indeed the language of statistics is rarely as objective as we imagine. The way statistics are presented, their arrangement in a particular way in tables, the juxtaposition of sets of figures, in itself reflects the judgment of the author about what is significant and what is trivial in the situation which the statistics portray. No figure by itself is of any significance, it only comes to have meaning when related to some other figure. I always remember how, when I was a student of economics in the 1930s, two of my teachers, with rather different views, used the unemployment percentage figures to attempt to create in our minds a picture of the efficiency of the working of the economic system. One used to tell us how inefficient our economic system was and tried to drive home his point by saying that for many years unemployment had been more than 20 per cent of the labour force, and in no year since the end of the post-war boom had it been less than 10 per cent. The other, concerned to demonstrate the resilience of the economic system in changing adverse circumstances, used to tell us that in most years since the end of the war the resources of the community had been employed to at least 90 per cent, and even in the worst years never less than 80 per cent. This was my first lesson in the objectivity of statistics!

One of the attractive features of economic statistics is that it makes possible, indeed is a positive inducement, to dealing in aggregates. It is so easy to add up employment figures, figures of foreign trade, or of incomes, and deals in totals of man-power, exports, imports, consumption, investment, etc.

The development of aggregative economic analysis receives powerful reinforcement from the increasing availability of statistics, and in turn induces the use of economic statistics in broad categories. It is fatally easy, by this means, to overlook the divergent trends which such aggregates conceal, and to see trends in aggregates which are merely the accidental results of important varying movements in sub-categories. It is not easy statistically to portray the great variation in skill, training capacity, experience, aptitude and zeal for work of the labour force of any country; and as a consequence we tend to deal in figures of man-power, analysed, at most, by industry. It is fatally easy, as a consequence, to drop into the habit of treating these groups as homogeneous units, for even when we recognize the falsity of such an assumption, we can make little allowance for this in our statistical analysis.

It would of course be very much easier to understand economic events if they merely reflected the interaction of a handful of measurable fundamental relationships. And since it is now so easy apparently to describe an economic system in terms of a few broad statistical aggregates, this in itself may give us the illusion that we can explain economic events in this simple way. The invention of social accounting, so fruitful and beneficial in many ways, has in this respect been especially ensnaring.

I now turn to the second main characteristic of the language of statistics, the air of precision and accuracy which inevitably goes with description of events in terms of figures. Some would argue that this is not a necessary characteristic of the language, that estimates can be given in round figures, indicating the lack of precision, or that figures can be quoted with margins of error small or large, indicating inaccuracy and error in the fundamental data. But I am not persuaded by these arguments. Firstly, because figures are so easily abstracted from the text which may explain their tenuous basis; secondly because, even if a margin of error is given in the original publication, a figure and its margin of error are so easily parted. And lastly, and perhaps most important of all, figures, by their very nature, even if qualified in the text or quoted with margins of error, inevitably convey an impression of precision.

We all know that in economic statistics particularly, true

precision, comparability and accuracy is extremely difficult to achieve, and it is for this reason that the language of economic statistics is so difficult to handle. How to use a language which by its very nature implies objectivity, precision and accuracy, in such a way that the subjective element of judgment, imprecision and inaccuracy are fully taken into account? It is because this task is so difficult and so rarely achieved that statistics are frequently referred to as 'the hard facts', and yet we talk of three kinds of lies—'lies, damn lies, and statistics'. Or we say, mindful of the ease with which one can be misled in the use of the language, that 'you can prove anything with statistics'. It is, however, interesting to note that it is frequently just those who express this scepticism of statistics in principle, who are most easily taken in by a distorted or misleading statistical argument. The art of using the language of figures correctly is not to be over-impressed by the apparent air of accuracy, and yet to be able to take account of error and inaccuracy in such a way as to know when, and when not, to use the figures. This is a matter of skill, judgment, and experience, and there are no rules and short cuts in acquiring this expertness. But there are some general lessons worth while learning and some devices for demonstrating error and reliability, and I now turn to consider some of these.

First, however, I would like to comment on the technique which consists of 'looking the difficulties squarely in the face and then passing on'. This is a common habit of economists, econometricians, financial journalists and even economic statisticians themselves, and arises partly from ignorance and partly from an irritation and impatience with all the qualifications and cautions that commonly accompany the statistics they use. They also have a terrifying suspicion that, if they took all these qualifications and cautions seriously, they would not be able to use the statistics for the purpose they have in mind. This would in their view be obviously ridiculous. And this disaster can only be avoided by the bland assumption that the 'statistics' are reasonably reliable for the purpose in hand. The commonest, and apparently most respectable, way of reconciling this conflict between the unreliability of the figures and the preference to believe that the unreliability does not matter for the particular use one has in mind, is to pay one's full respects before the shrine of statistical respectability by explaining in some detail the inaccuracies and unreliability of the statistics one is going to use, and then proceeding to use them as if error did not affect their use. One might then make a final kow-tow in the direction of the statisticians by concluding the argument with such a statement as, 'the error in the statistics must be borne in mind in assessing the reliability of this analysis'. Alternative formulations of the same pricedure are to refer to the tenuous basis of the figures and then to state, without any evidence, 'but they probably give the right order of magnitude', and then to proceed blandly as if there were no error in the figures at all. This attitude to error and unreliability is implicit in most econometric analysis of the determinants of general economic activity and in forecasts of inflationary and deflationary gaps. This attitude to error and unreliability is very common in the use, for example, of the official figures of savings. It is regularly pointed out by the user that they are unreliable, being a residual difference between two large magnitudes, and then one goes on to discuss changes in savings as if, in fact, these figures could be relied on.

There is a similar, though more sinister and dangerous, technique of 'facing the difficulty squarely and then passing on', in the use of secondary statistics. By secondary statistics I mean statistics which attempt to measure changes in some important theoretical concept either in statistical or economic theory. I have in mind such constructs as production and price index numbers or the national income. For here there is not merely the question of the reliability of the basic data which we use, but also of the meaning and measurability of the concepts we have in mind. The clearest examples of this problem are in index numbers. There has been much theoretical examination in recent years of the meaning and significance of what we measure in index numbers, and most of this analysis leads to the conclusion, that, except in very special and most unusual circumstances, it is not possible to give any significant meaning to index numbers of real national income, production or prices. At best, even if we had all the necessary statistical information, we would have a range of index numbers without any clear criteria for choosing between them. Index numbers are, in fact, a device for measuring what is theoretically immeasurable. And, if I may use such obviously contradictory terms, the more immeasurable theoretically, the more desirable they become statistically. When changes in production, or prices, are small, the theoretical objection to index numbers is perhaps least, but then we are not particularly interested in them; but if changes are large the theoretical objection is great, but we feel the need for them most. Now index numbers play such a vital role in economic and statistical analysis that the thought of being deprived of them is unbearable. We have all acquired the very convenient habit of keeping our ideas in two strictly divided compartments. We all know the theoretical objections and limitations, but when it comes to using index numbers we manage, Freudian-like, to forget all these. Preferring to believe, if challenged, that for the particular use we have in mind, the theoretical limitations and qualifications can be ignored. We all succumb to this temptation.

Or take another example: figures of the national income at factor cost analysed by the main sectors of the economy. These purport to measure the contribution which various sectors—industry, agriculture, distribution, Government administration, etc., make to the total national product. We know, if we consider the theoretical background to such figures, that no precise meaning can be given to them unless we make very stringent assumptions, for example that all factors are paid their marginal product (whatever that may mean), that there is perfect competition and constant costs. Otherwise what meaning can be attached to the proposition that the contribution of industry to the national product is, say, seven times that of agriculture? Certainly unless these stringent assumptions are made we cannot assume even at the margin that, say, £100 million of resources from industry would, if transferred to agriculture, add £100 million to the net product of agriculture. We know all this and when we discuss it in terms of economic theory think it obvious and elementary. But how quickly we conveniently forget it and push it into the back of our minds when we come to juggle with the national income figures!

There are two standard replies to these criticisms and objections that I have been raising. The first is for the user to defend himself by saying, 'well I explained the basis of my figures and their unreliability, didn't I?', as if having covered himself in this way, even if only in an obscure footnote, he then has every right to use the statistics as he wishes. The assumption is that it is up to the reader or user of the results of the analysis to assess the effects on it of the error in the basic data. The second standard reply is rather more cunning and ensnaring. It consists in admitting, perhaps even frequently referring to, the unsatisfactory nature of the data, but arguing that they are the best that exist and arguing by implication 'that any figure, however rough, is surely better than no figure'. This is a very widely held view among statisticians and economists. I do not agree with it, but must admit that when I argue with my colleagues about it I am usually in a minority of one. The reason I disagree is because, as I explained before, the use of figures, in my view, inevitably carries with it an implication of precision. If, therefore our basic information, or the conceptual difficulties involved, really preclude such precision as is implied by the use of the quantities, it seems to me better to use no figure at all. In such circumstances any figure however much surrounded with qualifications and limitations, even if quoted as a range, is more misleading than enlightening; and it is better to describe the information we have in other terms.

I feel that this is the position in international comparisons of national income per head; that, in truth, except, as an illusion, these add nothing to our information and are likely, if anything, positively to mislead. For where the differences in national income per head come out to be very great, the conceptual difficulties involved in attaching significance to the comparisons, because of the entirely different institutional and economic situations being compared, are such that we can attach little meaning to the quantitative difference. What does it mean, for example, to say that the national income per head of the United States is forty times as great as that of the Philippines (I take this figure from the United National Statistical Office publication on national and per capita incomes), or that the national income per head of Poland is seven times that of Saudi-Arabia? Would we not give a better and truer picture of the state of our knowledge and the difficulty of making such comparisons if we merely said that the United States standard of living is very much higher than that of the Philippines, a fact that we know without making any comparisons of national income statistics? And, unfortunately, when the figures only show a small margin of difference they are also unreliable. For even the most accurate figures of national income have a substantial margin of error, and when we come to compare two countries in real terms, whether we use actual or estimated parity exchange rates or more detailed investigations of comparative prices in the two countries, the margin of error in the final result is very substantial. I would myself attach very little significance to the margin in national income per head, for example, shown between Denmark (689 US 1949 dollars) and Belgium (582).

The most important and frequently stressed prescription for avoiding pitfalls in the use of economic statistics, is that one should find out before using any set of published statistics, how they have been collected, analysed and tabulated. This is especially important, as you know, when the statistics arise not from a special statistical enquiry, but are a by-product of law or administration. Only in this way can one be sure of discovering what exactly it is that the figures measure, avoid comparing the non-comparable, take account of changes in definition and coverage, and as a consequence not be misled into mistaken interpretations and analysis of the events which the statistics portray. Everyone recognizes the need to understand the administrative and legal aspects of unemployment and national insurance administration in this country before using the unemployment figures, to know something of the administrative procedures of Her Majesty's Customs and Excise before using the foreign trade statistics in the Trade and Navigation Accounts.

Although I agree wholeheartedly with this advice, there are serious difficulties in following it. First the task is enormous. If one used statistics only after examining in great detail the basis on which they were collected, and the administrative and legal procedures they reflected, then the statistics that each of us could use would be very limited indeed. For even the economic statistician who is prepared to specialize in this field cannot hope, himself, to cover more than a minute part of the subject. One only has to look at that valuable series of papers sponsored by the Royal Statistical Society on 'Sources and Nature of the Statistics of the United

Kingdom' to see the enormous range of knowledge implied in such a venture. And, unfortunately, it is difficult in this field to take much advantage of the division of labour. For the knowledge that you get from a detailed study of the sources and methods used in compiling the statistics, cannot be summarized and communicated in terms of a statistical assessment of error or degree of reliability, which can be easily used by others. This is partly because where statistics are a by-product of administration or law, one cannot give them a once and for all assessment of reliability. The reliability will change with changing circumstances, and one can only be alive to the effect of such changing circumstances by being steeped oneself in the knowledge of the detailed administrative process from which the statistics are derived. It would not have been possible, for example, for someone from a study of the administration of the National Insurance Acts in 1948 and 1949 to have arrived at an assessment valid for all time of the reliability, accuracy and significance of the unemployment figures published by the Ministry of Labour. One could not have foreseen the peculiar effects on the figures of unemployment, of the operation of the Unemployment Insurance system in the cotton slump of 1952.

But this ideal is in any case impracticable; for large sections of official statistics it is difficult, if not impossible, to discover the detailed basis of compilation. We know, for example, very little of the detailed processes by which the Ministry of Labour arrives at its estimates of working population. At best, we have to proceed by a process of detection and surmise.

This difficulty, both in principle and in practice, of knowing in detail the basis of all the statistics we use has a peculiar but striking result. It might be reasonable to expect that the more we know about any set of statistics, the greater the confidence we would have in using them, since we would know in which directions they were defective; and that the less we know about a set of figures, the more timid and hesitant we would be in using them. But, in fact, it is the exact opposite which is normally the case; in this field, as in many others, knowledge leads to caution and hesitation, it is ignorance that gives confidence and boldness. For knowledge about any set of statistics reveals the possibility of error at every stage of the statistical process; the difficulty of getting complete coverage in the returns, the difficulty of framing answers precisely and unequivocally, doubts about the reliability of the answers, arbitrary decisions about classification, the roughness of some of the estimates that are made before publishing the final results. Knowledge of all this, and much else, in detail, about any set of figures makes one hesitant and cautious, perhaps even timid, in using them. But if all one sees and knows is the final result, especially if published in neat, well laid out statistical tables, printed on good quality paper and made up in expensive binding, how tempting it is to assume that the figures are probably quite reliable, and how frequently we succumb to the temptation.

I do not myself think that this picture is in any way exaggerated. We all use the figures of the balance of payments for the United Kingdom in 1938 with great confidence because we do not really know how they are compiled; we are much more careful in using the recent figures, for a mere glance at the White Papers gives us some idea of the process of estimation involved in providing the figures, and the frequent revisions of back figures serves to impress on us the margins of error that there must be in the current figures. I am sure that most British statisticians treat United States statistics as more accurate than they do those for this country, largely through ignorance of the basis of most US figures. The statisticians at international organizations such as OEEC and the UN always use the national statistics of their constituent members with greater confidence than the national statisticians of each of the countries concerned. The econometricians remote from the sources of the statistics they employ are the prime examples of the bold approach in the use of economic statistics.

One of the reasons for this lack of discrimination in the use of economic statistics, is that official statistics are usually published without any indication of relative degrees of reliability, and that there are no cautions for the unwary reader. Thus, all the figures of employment published in the Ministry of Labour Gazette every month, whether they be about the total working population, employment in distribution or employment in manufacturing industries, are published in exactly the same way, as if they were subject to the same degree of accuracy or error. Is there any way of remedying this, short of suggesting that the official statisticians ought to publish the basis of their figures in the greatest detail and anyone who wants to use them should first become completely familiar with this detail? For this extreme position would be a course of despair and would imply that 'statistics are only for the statistician', and even then, I might add, only for the good statistician. Then the statisticians themselves might be obsessed and mesmerized by the qualifications, inaccuracies, guesses, and changes in definition in the figures of which they have specialist knowledge, and become so hesitant that they are unwilling to see the figures used for any purpose whatsoever. But whether this is the right remedy or not, it will not be adopted, for the non-specialist will insist on having access to the figures and using them for his own purposes.

Is there then no way of meeting these difficulties? Various devices are used to safeguard against misuse and others have frequently been suggested. The commonest are merely 'cover' devices for the statistician, they do not really help the user, but enable the statistician to claim that he has given the necessary warnings. Typical devices are obscure warning footnotes or statements that figures are 'not comparable' or 'not strictly comparable', although I have never been able to puzzle out the significance of this fine distinction; putting some figures in brackets, or putting a line across a column to indicate discontinuity in coverage. Most of these devices merely serve to irritate the reader and are largely ignored by him when he comes to use the figures.

A suggestion frequently made and used by some, is that statistics should always be published with an estimated margin of error or graded A, B, C, D, according to their reliability. This latter device is used by the distinguished Irish statistician, Mr Geary, in the Irish statistics of national income and expenditure. He uses 'A' for firm figures, 'B' for 'good estimates', 'C' for rough estimates, and 'D' for conjectures or 'pure guess'. This device is also used by Mrs Chapman in her recently published elaborate analysis of wages and salaries in the United Kingdom between the wars.

The publication of official statistics with margins of error, which is not, of course, at present generally done in this country, raises many difficulties. First of all the assessment of a margin of error would imply more accurate knowledge of the true error in the figures than is usually possessed by the official statistician. Indeed the kind of information which would usually enable one to quote figures of error, would itself enable one to reduce the extent of error in the figures. One of the elements of error in using the Board of Inland Revenue figures for national income calculations is the extent of evasion. A precise knowledge of the extent of evasion, apart from enabling Her Majesty's Commissioners to take more effective steps to prevent evasion in future, would enable the Central Statistical Office to eliminate this error in their use of the figures. It is because they do not know the extent of evasion at all accurately that there is inevitably a margin of error, on this account, in the income figures. Margins of error for this kind of reason, and those due to inaccuracies in filling up statistical returns, must inevitably be a matter of judgment. It might, however, be possible to do something to make the assessment more objective by undertaking sample analysis to check the 'real error' in a few cases, and then work from the sample to assess the error in the population as a whole.

Frequently the margins of error quoted are merely assumed margins of error or implied margins of error in derived statistics, on assumptions about error in the statistics from which they are derived. One could assess the margin of error in the figures of personal saving in the national income blue book on assumptions about the error in the statistics of income and expenditure from which they are derived. Thus, for example, if one assumed that there was a margin of error of 1 per cent either way in the figures of total personal income and total personal expenditure, one could work out for 1952 that this would give a margin of error of $\pm$ 50 per cent in the personal savings figures for that year. This is truly a striking way of demonstrating the wide margin of error in a residual derived by difference from two large figures, each of which is fairly accurate. But it gives us no basis for assuming that the $\pm$ 50 per cent is a good estimate of the error in the figure of personal saving, since we have no warranty for an assumption that the margin of error in the figures of expenditure and personal income are 1 per cent. Or, sometimes, the difference between two alternative sources for statistics is assumed to measure the margins of error in each. Thus figures of employment collected by the Ministry of Labour and in the Census of Production are often used in this way. But to calculate margins of error in this way, is of course, pure assumption and guesswork.

The 'reliability' rating system also has its difficulties. As with the assessment of margins of error, it depends a great deal on individual subjective judgment. What one person might rank as 'C'—a rough estimate, another might rank as 'D'—a pure guess. Some consistency of standard might be achieved where the rating was done by one person who knew all the statistics fairly well himself, but to apply this system to all British official statistics would mean allowing a large number of people to do their rating independently of each other.

A more fundamental objection to the reliability rating system is that reliability cannot usefully be assessed in an absolute sense, separately from the particular use which is being made of the figure. Thus figures of British exports and imports might be classified as 'A', if one were using them to compare year to year movements, but only as 'B' in measuring the significance of month to month changes. Or the separate estimates of population, deaths and births published by the Registrar-General for Scotland, might all be rated as 'A' for the analysis of changes in population, mortality and fertility, but only as 'B', 'C' or even 'D' if they were going to be used to derive figures of migration to or from Scotland. Clearly in view of the large range of uses to which any set of statistics may be put, a reliability rating is often of little value to the user; although I agree that it is better than nothing.

It will by now be clear that I do not think that there is any easy way of learning the correct use of the language of economic statistics. I am impressed by the difficulty of avoiding misuse, and the frequent occasions on which the language can easily be more misleading than enlightening. There are clearly no simple rules which will enable one to become an efficient expert in the use of the language. But, as in learning most other languages, practice in using it is the most important element; no amount of study of grammar and syntax can take the place of practice. I have tried hard in the last few years to work out some general guiding principles which I could pass on to my students to help them to acquire a facility in reading, writing and speaking this language of figures, but when I am honest with myself I have to admit that on the whole I have failed.

The ease with which figures can be misinterpreted can perhaps best be illustrated by an example. I always set my students a question giving a table of figures and taking them to write an essay on it. The question I set in a recent paper was a table based on the 1951 Census one per cent. sample results, showing the distribution of the population of this country by main age groups, sex, and marital conditions, showing separately the numbers single, married, widowed and divorced. Since the Census relates only to the population in this country, the number of married women shown in the Census results was rather larger than the number of married men, and you will of course know that the difference was largely accounted for by the number of married men, in the Armed Forces and Merchant Navy, overseas on the night of the Census. This was a minor feature of the table, but it was seized on as of great significance by many of the candidates. Some commented that this showed conclusively that 'polygamy was far more common in this country than was generally believed'; others that clearly 'many women liked to think and say they were married even though they were not'. Very few gave the correct explanation. Such are the hazards and pitfalls in using and interpreting this most difficult and peculiar language.

7

Statistics as a Basis for Policy[1]

IN the debate and discussion that precedes and surrounds the many important decisions in the economic and social sphere taken by the Government and other public authorities, statistics have come to play an apparently greater and greater role in recent years. No economic issue is raised without batteries of figures being produced supporting or opposing a particular line of action, and more and more reliance is put on statistical analysis in trying to get the correct answer.

It is never easy to discover after the event what forces actually determined the decision which was taken in particular circumstances, and dispassionate study of public decision-taking is still in its infancy. Yet there is sufficient evidence to make a discussion of the role that statistics play in this process interesting and possibly profitable. It is impossible to deal with the whole field of economic decision-taking in a short article, and I confine my attention to three major spheres, all of considerable current importance. First, long-term production and investment planning by public authorities, particularly by nationalized undertakings; second, the allocation of expenditure and over-all control of investment by the central government; and third, the conduct of general economic policy designed to keep the country on an even keel.

In recent years many public authorities have tried to estimate by statistical analysis the long-term demand for the products of the industry they run, as a basis for drawing up production or investment plans. Such plans have been a regular feature of the work of the National Boards for coal, gas and electricity; and the central government has encouraged, if not actually required, the steel industry to draw up such plans. The Cotton Board has made similar estimates from time to time

[1] *Lloyds Bank Review*, July 1954.

about the long-term demand for the products of the cotton industry; but they are not so important as those for coal or steel, since the Cotton Board exercises no direct control over production and investment in the industry.

In principle, the problems that face the Coal Board, the Steel Board, or the Cotton Board in attempts to estimate future demand are the same as those which face any single firm which tries consciously to work out some basis for deciding long-term investment and production policy. And where a single firm dominates an industry, the problems are much the same in practice. All such estimates are bound to contain a very large element of assumption or hazardous guesswork. However much statistical analysis is undertaken, no final certain figure of future demand can ever be arrived at. Inevitably, the decision about how much plant and production to plan implies a substantial element of risk-taking, and the decision about what risk to take is one of the most important functions performed by the businessman. Public authorities can no more avoid taking such risks, either consciously or by default, than can a private firm.

It is true that there was for a time a widespread view— it may still be widespread—that the central government, the nationalized boards, and their servants in Whitehall have special knowledge and techniques which would enable them to narrow these risks very substantially, if not to eliminate them altogether. Indeed, one of the arguments frequently put forward in support of nationalization or public control was that output and investment could then be planned on a co-ordinated long-term basis, instead of being accidentally determined by the vagaries of market forces. And it was usually implied that statistical analysis of major long-term trends, which either could not or would not be undertaken by single firms or private industries, would provide the basis for such investment and production planning.

The experience of the Coal Board provides an interesting example of an attempt to draw up a long-term plan on the basis of such statistical analysis. In the *Plan for Coal*,[1] the National Coal Board explains how it tried to estimate the level of output for which the Board ought to provide for the years 1961–5, at that time about ten to fifteen years ahead.

[1] Published in October 1950.

Even a cursory glance at Chapter III, dealing with 'Demand', reveals the large number of assumptions that are involved, even if not consciously made, in any estimates of future demand for coal: assumptions about the future level of output in industries consuming coal, the course of efficiency in using coal, the competition of alternative fuels, domestic and export demand and, most troublesome of all, the effect on all these of varying assumptions about the likely future trend of coal prices.

How do statistics and statistical analysis help the Board, if at all, to decide what are the right or the best assumptions to make? In assessing future industrial demand for coal, the Plan starts with a crude comparison between the movement of coal consumption by industry and the level of industrial production between 1946 and 1950. It then proceeds, 'assuming present trends continued for only another five years, the coal consumed by industry and public utilities might be expected to rise to 155 million tons', compared with 140 million tons in 1950. 'Adding 60 million tons for coal consumed at collieries, by householders and miscellaneous consumers, the total inland demand would be 215 million tons', compared with actual consumption of 196 million tons in 1950. This is an extrapolation only five years ahead; a continuation of the projection for fifteen years would have given a figure of 245 million tons. This seems to have frightened the Coal Board, since the calculation is not even given for the fifteen-year period. But we are warned how dangerous it would be to project such a short-term trend into the future. An analysis of pre-war trends, we are told, 'gives an inland demand in the long run of not more than 190 million tons'. Then comes the prize statement that 'the true estimate probably lies somewhere between the two figures' [of 190 and 215] and 'the Board have, for purposes of their first plan, estimated the inland demand at between 205 million and 215 million tons'. No evidence is produced to support this assessment of probability, and the figure of 215 million tons, which was first given as an estimate for *five* years ahead (i.e. for 1955) is now treated without explanation as the upward limit of consumption for 1961-5.

The plan explains that this estimate of total demand is based not only on an analysis of past trends but also takes into account 'the known or probable developments of the main industries'. There follows some discussion of the likely level of demand in gas, steel, railways and electricity. In these cases the plan virtually takes over the estimates of demand made by each industry, although the grounds for hesitation and doubt are emphasized. Thus, 'the long-term demand for coal by coke ovens depends primarily on how much metallurgical coke is required for steel making, and the future demand for steel in the markets of the world is not easy to assess'. The statistical evidence brought forward in support of the estimates for particular industries is much too tenuous and uncertain to be thought of as corroborating the earlier estimate on the global basis.

This still leaves coal exports, obviously extremely difficult to forecast. Here we are enlightened by the platitudinous statements which so frequently occur in these exercises. 'The amount that can be expected depends upon the share of the trade which the British coal industry can win in competition with foreign suppliers of coal and other forms of fuel.' Figures of exports in the inter-war years are quoted, but these are not very relevent. After some disussion of various aspects of export possibilities, none expressed in statistical terms, the section concludes 'taking one thing with another, the Board have assessed the overseas demand as lying between 25 and 35 million tons a year'. This, together with the estimate of 205–15 million tons for inland demand, gives the total of 230–50 million tons, the middle figure of 240 millions being used in the rest of the document.

Is it necessary to demonstrate that in this case statistical analysis has hardly served to reduce uncertainty and risk to any great extent? No one, least of all apparently the Coal Board, would treat the final figure of 240 million tons as a firm basis for planning. Indeed, it is significant that the plan explains that any alteration in the figure of 240 million, say an upward revision, would not affect the action to be taken under the plan, since 'the programme for the next 15 years is in any case a maximum'.

Two years after the publication of the *Plan for Coal* another estimate of the future demand for coal was made by the Committee on National Policy for Use of Fuel and Power Resources,[1] generally known as the 'Ridley Committee'. The

[1] Cmd. 8647, September 1952.

Ridley Committee, much bolder than the Coal Board, arrived at a set of estimates for coal consumption in 1959-63 by rigorously working out to their final conclusion a set of assumptions about the future level of output in each major industry, the relation between output and the use of fuel, and the competition of alternative fuels, especially oil. The estimate of total inland coal demand arrived at by the Ridley Committee is considerably higher than the figure given in the Coal Plan—232 millions compared with 205–15 millions —even though the Ridley Committee's estimates are for a slightly earlier period.[1] One of the major assumptions which determine the Ridley Committee's final result is the rate of increase in industrial output, about which the Coal Plan was so cautious and evasive. The Ridley Committee assumed a cumulative rate of increase of 4 per cent per annum in steel production and in production in the main sectors of industry. Allowance is made for improved fuel efficiency. This is not specified for iron and steel, but is taken to result in an increase in fuel consumption of 3 per cent per annum in the rest of industry, which is well in excess of what was implied in the Coal Plan.

The Ridley Committee recognizes 'that many of our assumptions may turn out to be wide of the mark, and if they do, the effect on demand for fuel will be significant'. If industrial production increased by only 2 per cent and fuel efficiency by $\frac{1}{2}$ per cent (instead of the assumed 4 per cent and 1 per cent) the estimate of demand in 1959–63 would be reduced by 15 million tons; if production increased by 6 per cent and fuel efficiency by 1 per cent, the estimate would be exceeded by 15 to 20 million tons. Taking these two alternative assumptions quoted by the Ridley Committee would give an estimate for inland consumption between 215 and 250 million tons. Hardly a basis for planning, since it merely tells us that the risks involved in estimates for the future are very large. Yet the Ridley Committee uses the single figure of 232 for inland consumption, takes over the Coal Plan figures of 25 to 35 million for exports and gives 257-67 million tons as its estimate of total annual coal requirements in the period 1959–63.

Here, then, we have three sets of estimates: the Coal

[1] Average 1959–63, compared with 1961–5 used in the *Plan for Coal*.

Board's of 230–50 million tons, the Ridley Committee's of 257–67 million and, taking the Ridley Committee's illustrative alternative assumptions about the rate of increase in industrial production and fuel efficiency, an even wider range between 240–85 million tons. The substantial difference between these estimates reflects the simple fact that if we make different assumptions we will get different results, and the wider the range of alternative assumptions the bigger the difference between the final estimates. No statistical analysis will give us a criterion for selecting with confidence between the various alternative assumptions used in this case. There is no objective test that can be used to discover in advance which is the best set of estimates. The plausibility to different people of widely varying assumptions merely serves to illustrate our uncertainty about the future, and the big differences between the final estimates should make it clear that we have to take big risks if we want to plan investment or production a long way ahead.

It may well be said that while all this is true, the Coal Board nevertheless has to decide how much coal to produce and how much to invest in order to expand production in the future. This is undoubtedly so, and the Board may feel it necessary to assure themselves and the public that they are taking their decisions on an apparently rational assessment of all the evidence. And what more convincing way of doing this than by discussing the issue in statistical terms. But it would be misleading to think that this examination of the statistical evidence eliminates or even appreciably reduces the risks that the Coal Board, as any private business, has to take in planning for the future. The statistical analysis, by showing the implications of varying assumptions, perhaps plays a useful role in revealing the magnitude of the risks involved. It does little, if anything, to reduce the risks or to help in deciding which is the best risk to take.

Coal has been discussed as an interesting case and because information in some detail has been published about the basis of estimates of future demand. The published evidence for other industries, such as steel, which have undertaken production or investment planning since the war, is much more limited, but tends to confirm the conclusions drawn from the coal example. In all these cases the estimate of demand is built up from a series of assumptions, the choice of assumptions being largely a matter of judgment and temperament. The validity of the particular assumptions used is not demonstrated; indeed usually it is not even discussed.

It is true that once you have decided what figure to go for, what risk to take, it is quite easy to build up a statistical picture of requirements to back up the decisions that have been taken. It is merely a matter of choosing the appropriate assumptions. And this may be quite useful in exposing the assumptions and, therefore, the risk implied in the course of action that is being followed. But the unwary reader may easily be led to believe that such a statistical statement actually demonstrates that the right risks are being taken.

III

The second sphere of decision-taking chosen for examination is that of central government activity in allocating expenditure and controlling the level and distribution of investment. Here the regularly recurring questions which demand answers are such as: what should the Government spend on education, health, pensions or other social services? What on defence? How many houses should the Government plan to build or subsidize? What proportion of the national income should be invested? Which particular avenues of investment should be encouraged and which discouraged?

It is important to realize that in the actual process of decision-taking, these questions normally have to be answered only in terms of a little more or a little less. Once the Government is committed to expenditure on some particular service, the question whether the total expenditure on the service is worth while is rarely debated as an issue of practical politics. The real question for decision is not usually, therefore, how much should the Government spend in total on this or that service, but how much more or less should be spent next year. Most of the questions that have to be answered relate to relatively small marginal adjustments. But occasionally —for example, in arguments before deciding to introduce the National Health Service—issues about the worthwhileness of expenditure are raised on a grander scale.

How do statistics and statistical analysis help in providing answers to these questions? Let us take housing policy as an example. Should the Government plan to subsidize 250,000, 300,000, or 350,000 houses a year? How decide on the right answer? It is sometimes suggested that a detailed statistical analysis of present housing conditions and needs would provide the answer. How does one decide on 'housing needs'? The usual answer is in the unhelpful form that 'enough houses should be built to house everybody adequately'. What is the criterion of adequacy? A house for every family? How big a house? How is a family to be defined? How quickly is such a desirable state of affairs to be reached: in five, ten or twenty years? No amount of statistical analysis can give answers to such questions.

This does not mean that statistics are of no help in resolving issues of housing policy. Although statistical analysis cannot give a direct answer to the question how many houses to build, it can fill gaps in our knowledge about present housing conditions and expose the implications of alternative house-building programmes. Thus, an analysis of the results of the 1951 Census of Population may show how many small families or single persons are living in houses on their own. Social surveys of housing conditions may throw light on the extent of overcrowding, although this is itself an ambiguous term. A statistical analysis, by income, occupation and size of family, of the people who go into new houses might reveal some surprising facts about the sections of the population that are reaping the main benefit from the policy of subsidizing houses on a large scale. An examination of the changing conditions of old houses might reveal some of the effects of rent restriction. All such information and much else is without doubt relevant for housing policy; for although none of it answers the question at issue directly, it brings to light facts which are relevant to the decision. We cannot rationally decide how many houses to subsidize without having some knowledge of who will benefit, even though when we have such knowledge it will not tell us unequivocally how many houses to subsidize.

The use of statistics in argument about expenditure on education is much the same. Should we spend more or less on education? Discussion of this issue is frequently conducted with statistical arguments. Figures are quoted about the size of classes, the age of buildings, the proportion of children

I

beyond fifteen receiving an education, the proportion of the population attending universities, the supply of school teachers, and so on. But accumulation of statistical information of this kind will not give us a direct answer to the question: should we spend more or less? Just as with housing, we cannot take a rational decision without such information. We cannot sensibly decide whether we think more or less should be spent, unless we have some appreciation of what is achieved with the present level of expenditure, and how this would be affected by spending more or less. But the information, no matter how accurate and voluminous, cannot by itself settle the issue, for, as we know, two people given exactly the same information may take quite different views whether educational expenditure ought to be raised or cut.

IV

The use of statistics in the control of investment by the central government raises different issues. It is now generally acknowledged that there are no objective criteria by which the Government can decide what is the right amount of investment in total. But it is still sometimes argued that it is possible by statistical analysis to decide on the distribution of investment. If the Government in its control over investment merely wants to imitate market procedure and to select the lines of investment that will pay best, then it might try to work out rates of return on the various projects submitted to it and use such rates as the criteria for selecting which to approve. Even on this basis, however, prospective rates of return could be calculated only within very wide margins, representing the essential risk involved in such forecasting and, as with estimates of future coal and steel requirements, statistical investigation might expose and illustrate these risks but is unlikely to narrow them.

Usually, Government control of investment does not merely try to imitate market procedures; indeed, the very purpose of Government control is to prevent ordinary market forces being the criterion of distribution. The controlling authority tries to select on the basis of the public interest or of social priorities. It is extremely difficult to see how social priorities or social rates of return can be measured statistically.

How does one compare statistically the social rate of return from building more houses with the social rate of return from more investment on road building and repair? Or compare the social rate of return from additional investment in the coal industry with investment in engineering or textiles?

Whether or not it is possible to measure social rates of return statistically, there is in any case little evidence that such calculations ever played an important role in the deliberations of the Capital Issues Committee and the Investments Programme Committee. Little has been published about the proceedings of these two important committees and the criteria which they used in arriving at their decisions, but I suspect that the allocation of investment is much better thought of as the result of political and administrative struggles and pressures, than as a rational choice determined by the statistical measurement of rates of social return. Each industry or line of investment is the administrative responsibility of some Government department and in the argument about the investment programme, each department fights for the interests for which it was responsible. Every argument would, of course, be used to demonstrate that the investment being sponsored is vital to the economy, because it would relieve a potential bottleneck, result in export expansion or dollar saving. The strength of this case, the efficiency with which it is presented, the power and energy of the Minister in charge, public pressure and generally accepted but vaguely expressed ideas of what is 'essential' and 'inessential', would all go to determine how each particular request for inclusion in the investment programme was treated.

No doubt argument before these committees would be dressed up in statistics, since every official knows that a statistical case always makes an impression. And if all those concerned play the statistical game correctly—especially if they are not sure that they are playing a game—then an apparent air of deciding the issues rationally in terms of quantitative estimates of the results of alternative lines of action may easily be maintained.

v

In the post-war period great claims were made for statistical analysis as a guide to a general employment policy. National income and expenditure was used as a device for forecasting whether in the coming year the economic situation would be inflationary or deflationary. In the more ambitious calculations the magnitude of the prospective inflationary or deflationary gap was also estimated. Such calculations, if reliable, would be of the greatest value to those responsible for decisions on economic policy, since they would help them to decide on the appropriate monetary or fiscal policy to adopt in order to prevent either over-full employment or unemployment from developing. Experience of the use of these calculations in the last few years has, however, demonstrated that the claims often made for them were much exaggerated.[1]

The essential forecasting element in national income and expenditure models lies in the assumptions about the future course of the most important aggregates which determine the level of production and expenditure. The final calculations merely reveal the implications of such assumptions. If one assumes an increased rate of construction and fixed investment, an attempt by business to accumulate stocks and greater buying pressure by consumers, it is hardly surprising that a forecast of income and expenditure will show inflationary pressure in the coming year. The crucial elements in the forecasts are those relating to investment and stock-building; only if the forecast of these is reliable will the rest of the calculation be significant.

The real problem, therefore, is how to forecast investment and stock-building. Should one make such forecasts by asking businessmen what their intentions are? If this is done, then one must bear in mind that businessmen, too, find it very difficult to foresee a change in direction. When investment and stock-building are rising appreciably they will tend to expect a continuation of the rise. This means that when the trend is markedly in an inflationary or deflationary direction one can forecast its continuance in the same direction for some time ahead and usually, but not always, be proved right. When the trend is not strong in either direction, on the other hand, it is difficult to see what is going to happen even for a short period ahead.

Even when one is confident about whether the direction is inflationary or deflationary, it is impossible to make a use-

[1] See my 'Planning by Economic Survey', *Economia*, August 1952.

ful forecast of the extent of the pressure expressed as a figure of the inflationary or deflationary gap; for, apart from other difficulties, the statistical errors in the estimates inevitably result in a figure for the gap with such wide limits that it is of little use to those who decide policy. A single figure for the gap can be given only if these errors are ignored.

In view of these difficulties in using the national income and expenditure forecasts, there is a strong case for paying more attention to statistics of the most sensitive indicators of economic change. Figures of order books, stocks, prices, overtime and short-time working and unemployment, if they are available promptly, are more likely to give us early warning of a change in business conditions than are national income and expenditure forecasts.

VI

Whatever the validity of these arguments about the limitations of the usefulness of statistics as a guide to action, it is apparent that statistics have popularly a much greater influence than this reasoning would suggest; for the use of statistics is certainly not confined to situations where it can really be shown that they narrow the range of uncertainty about the future or make rational action possible.

There is a demand for every issue of economic policy to be discussed in terms of statistics, and even those who profess a general distrust of statistics are usually more impressed by an argument in support of a particular policy if it is backed up by figures. There is a passionate desire in our society to see issues of economic policy decided on what we think are rational grounds. We rebel against any admission of the uncertainty of our knowledge of the future as a confession of weakness. What easier way to pander to this obsession than to have all issues debated in the scientific or pseudo-scientific language of statistics. The National Coal Board has perforce to draw up a Plan for Coal and make estimates of the demand for coal, even though such estimates are almost pure guess-work and play little part in influencing the Coal Board's action. The Ridley Committee would not dare, given the temper of modern economic thinking, to discuss fuel uses without first making an estimate of fuel requirements, even though such an estimate is based on a series of hazardous assumptions and is hardly necessary for a discussion of the major issues raised in the report. Education, social services, investment, defence, all have to be discussed in statistical terms. And the analysis of national income and expenditure gives us an apparently scientific basis—indeed a 'mathematical' basis which is more impressive—for making economic forecasts. Statistical tables, no matter what assumptions and guesses are involved in their calculation, so frequently appear to give a clearer, more assured and objective picture than can be given by a qualitative argument, necessarily imprecise and hedged round with qualifications.

This exaggerated influence of statistics resulting from willingness, indeed eagerness, to be impressed by the 'hard facts' provided by the 'figures', may play an important role in decision-taking. The Coal Board *has* to decide how much coal to produce, the Iron and Steel Federation how much new steel capacity to instal, the Government how much to spend on education and health, and what monetary and fiscal policy to follow. These authorities dare not admit, either to themselves or to the public, complete ignorance of rational criteria on which to base such decisions. What more tempting façade of rationality than the portrayal of some statistics that seem to point to policy in one direction rather than another? A private businessman may admit that some of his decisions, especially those about investment, are based on hunch, perhaps hardly to be distinguished from tossing a coin; but such admissions are inappropriate in public affairs.

No Chancellor of the Exchequer could introduce his proposals for monetary and fiscal policy in the House of Commons by saying 'I have looked at all the forecasts; some go one way, some another; so I decided to toss a coin and assume inflationary tendencies if it came down heads and deflationary if it came down tails'. No Government which revealed that its actions were decided in this fashion would command any public confidence. Indeed the Government itself might find it impossible to take decisions if it were really convinced that there was no evidence which pointed to a decision in one direction rather than in another. And statistics, however uncertain, can always apparently provide some basis. We are all willing to clutch at statistical straws and only too ready to be taken in by our own figures. Decisions must be taken, and even if it is exaggerated confidence in the statistics which helps the Government to decide rather than dither, should we complain?

Considered in this light there seem to be striking similarities between the role of economic statistics in our society and some of the functions which magic and divination play in primitive society. Magic in primitive society makes it possible for decisions on important issues to be taken where there is apparently no alternative rational basis of decision, given the knowledge and technique of the society. Magical oracles decide whether to hunt in one direction or another, whether or not on some particular occasion to go to war, or which husband to choose for your daughter. If such issues were left to be decided by argument and debate, wrangling would go on indefinitely with no decision ever taken. Since the chances of being right or wrong are about even in terms of the nature of these problems and the knowledge of the society, the important thing is that *some* decision should be taken. And what more efficient and sensible system than to settle the issue by magic?

We would not think of examining the entrails of a chicken, of consulting an oracle, or of asking a diviner to find out whether the recession in the United States is going to get worse or not. Yet much of the grubbing about among national income and expenditure figures, of the statistical model-building of the econometricians and the desperate search for trend signs in the latest statistics, bear striking similarities to primitive magic. The only trouble is that we have a very large number of magicians and witchdoctors.

Statistical magic, like its primitive counterpart, is a mystery to the public; and like primitive magic it can never be proved wrong. For if the diviner's advice appears to turn out wrong and no game is shot on the hunt, the war is lost, or the marriage a failure, it is not magic that is discredited. This merely demonstrates that the magic material used was inferior or that the diviner was wrong in his reading, or that his reading was wrongly interpreted. The oracle is never wrong; a mistake merely reinforces the belief in magic. It merely demonstrates conclusively that unless you do everything the right way you will get the wrong answer. So with us, bad forecasts rarely discredit statistical magic; they merely serve to demonstrate that the basic figures were bad, that the model was wrong or the statistician mistaken in his interpretation. Naturally, in these circumstances the result is misleading. But the lesson has been learnt; next time we shall use better figures, better models, and of course the statisticians and econometricians today would never make the silly misinterpretations made in 1944, 1945 or 1946. We are convinced, rightly or wrongly, that this is the scientific procedure and we are going to stick to it.

This analogy is not meant to lead to the conclusion that all uses of economic statistics are of this magical kind. Indeed, even in the few examples of decision-taking discussed earlier in this article, economic statistics are of much value even if not as useful as is often popularly supposed. If they do nothing more, attempts to estimate statistically the future demand for coal or steel serve to demonstrate the uncertainty of the future, and consequently provide a warning that we must be very wary in planning coal or steel output or investment. In issues of housing, education, and investment policy, statistics can provide us with an appreciation of the existing situation, and we can hope to show through statistical analysis some of the important implications and consequences of alternative possible lines of action.

It may often be possible to go a long way by intelligent use of statistics in exposing and preventing inconsistencies and contradictions in policy-decisions in different sectors of the economy. Thus, if the Government decides on a given house-building programme, one can attempt to work out the implications of this in terms of the production of bricks and the size of the building industry or the strength of the building labour force. Or if the Government were to consider building a number of new schools and raising the school-leaving age to sixteen, one could examine what this would imply in an increased supply of teachers and the consequential effect on the supply of university graduates to occupations other than teaching. This is one of the most useful roles for statistical analysis: to reveal the implications, and frequently the inconsistencies, in policy-decisions, and so attempt to ensure that the main lines of policy are in harmony and not in conflict.

Again, although it may be difficult to use national income

and expenditure analysis to forecast the economic climate, such analysis gives us a useful picture of the inter-relation of the main aggregates in the economy. Once inflationary pressure has been diagnosed there is no more powerful way of demonstrating the operation of such pressure than through a set of national income and expenditure accounts. And such accounts provide an excellent basis for discussing the alternative ways in which the Government might take action to counter such pressure.

There are, indeed, plenty of ways in which statistics can help in the process of decision-taking. But exaggerated claims for the role they can play merely serve to confuse rather than clarify issues of public policy, and lead those responsible for action to oscillate between over-confidence and over-scepticism in using them.

8

Statistics of the United Kingdom
Terms of Trade[1]

DURING recent years changes in the terms of trade have apparently played a major role in the fluctuating economic fortunes of the United Kingdom. Great attention has, therefore, been paid to the official statistics which measure the terms of trade. In this article I attempt to explain what it is exactly that the official statistics measure, and suggest further supplementary measures of the terms of trade to throw a more revealing light on the United Kingdom's foreign trade position. As will be seen, the statistical material which is used for these alternative measures is in many respects rough and unreliable, and the main purpose of this article is to suggest lines for further investigation and research rather than to put forward firm statistical conclusions.

The Official Statistics

Two sets of official statistics of the terms of trade are now published regularly. One on a monthly basis in the Board of Trade Journal and the Monthly Statistical Digest, the other on an annual basis in the Annual Abstract of Statistics. The monthly figures are derived from a comparison of index numbers of import and export prices; the annual ones from a comparison of index numbers of the average value of imports and exports. This difference in nomenclature is confusing since both sets of indices are in fact based on average value figures derived from the statistics of merchandise trade included in the Trade and Navigation Accounts.

The main difference between the two sets of indices is in the system of weighting used. The monthly figures use a fixed set of weights based on the trade of the previous year, and the comparison is made with that year as base. At present trade in 1953 is used for weighting, and changes in 'prices' and the terms of trade are compared with the average for 1953

[1] The Manchester School, September 1954.

as 100, figures being given monthly for 1953 as well as for the current year. The annual figures are not obtained directly from figures of average value but are derived from the indices of total value and volume which are calculated each quarter by the Board of Trade. Since the volume indices calculated by the Board of Trade are themselves base weighted, average value indices calculated by dividing changes in total value by such indices, will have moving weights related to the current distribution of trade. The quarterly and annual average value indices derived in this way, may therefore, reflect changes in the distribution of trade as well as changes in prices as such. And it was for this reason that the alternative set of indices, on a fixed weight basis, was introduced in 1946.

The base and weights for the monthly 'price' indices are changed each year to that of the previous year. Each set of indices runs for twelve months, but since figures are also given for the previous twelve months, there are monthly figures for two years on each successive base and system of weights. Monthly figures, with 1953 as base, are available for 1953 and 1954; with 1952 as base, for 1953 and 1952; with 1951 as base, for 1952 and 1951; and so on. The quarterly and annual average value indices are revised less frequently and at irregular intervals. Since the war three bases have been used in turn, 1938, 1947, and 1950. At each revision indices on the new base are calculated for one or two previous years, so there is a substantial overlapping period which makes it possible to link the indices together on a continuous basis. In the latest annual Statistical Abstract annual average value and terms of trade indices from 1935 to 1938, and 1947 to 1952, are linked together in this way to give a continuous series with 1950 = 100.

The methods used in calculating the two sets of indices, and the form of their publication, suggests that it is the official view that for short-period, especially month to month, comparisons of the terms of trade, the 'price' indices should be used, and that for longer period comparisons the average value indices should be used.[1] We are mainly concerned in

---

[1] The interpretation of comparisons of price or average value figures over a period of years with substantial changes in the distribution of trade raises the index number problem in an acute form, but this problem is outside the scope of the issues dealt with in this article.

this article with year by year changes in the terms of trade since the end of the war, and the official figures for the merchandise terms of trade given in Table 1 are those based on the 'average value' indices of imports and exports.

The Terms of Trade for all Foreign Transactions

Since the official figures are ultimately based on the Trade and Navigation Accounts, they cover merchandise trade only and reflect the basis of valuation used in those Accounts. Non-merchandise trade—shipping, travel, insurance, banking interest and dividends, Government expenditure—is an important element in the United Kingdom's overseas transactions, and it would be valuable if one could calculate the terms of trade allowing for changes in the prices of these items. For it certainly cannot be assumed without further evidence that the movements of the prices of non-merchandise items of imports and exports are on average the same as for the merchandise items. A more accurate calculation of the terms of trade would also value imports f.o.b., for the c.i.f. basis used in the Trade and Navigation Accounts includes many payments for freight, insurance and other services which are made to United Kingdom residents and not to foreigners.

There is in fact very little information about changes in the prices of the non-merchandise items in the balance of payments. Price information is published only for shipping services, and even this is for freight only. It would obviously be extremely difficult to measure the changing price of tourism, insurance, banking, and Government expenditure overseas; and the meaning to be attached to the changing price of income from dividends, interest and profits is by no means clear.

Estimates of price changes in the non-merchandise items of trade, apart from interest dividend and profit income, and of the c.i.f. price of merchandise imports, are, however, implied in some of the Tables now published in the annual Blue Book on National Income and Expenditure. The 'estimates of gross domestic expenditure at constant (1948) prices'[1] are obtained by adding up figures of revalued consumer expenditure, Government expenditure, capital expenditure and exports and subtracting imports. In this calculation,

[1] See National Income and Expenditure 1946–1952, p. viii.

therefore, we have a series of figures which revalues total imports and total exports—merchandise and non-merchandise—at constant 1948 prices. From other tables in the Blue Book or from the Balance of Payments White Paper we can get figures for the same definition of imports and exports at current prices. It is then a simple matter of arithmetic to derive the price indices for total imports and exports implied in the revalued figures used in the Blue Book.

It is not suggested that this calculation will yield figures of a high degree of reliability. They will merely show the price changes that are implied in the hazardous estimates that must be made by the Central Statistical Office in revaluing the invisible items of imports and exports at 1948 prices. Yet the results of such a calculation may be of interest (Table II). It will be seen that although the figures are not markedly different from those for merchandise trade only, these differences are not trivial.

The terms of trade on this wider basis rise by only 8·5 per cent[1] between 1948 and 1952 compared with a rise of 11 per cent on the narrower official definition.

Import Prices and the Prices of the Domestic Content of Exports
Both the measures of the terms of trade discussed so far compare the movement of import prices and export prices, as if the commodities exported and imported were unrelated to each other. In fact many items of British exports contain imported raw materials and the prices at which they are sold will therefore be influenced by raw material import prices. For many purposes it is important to be able to distinguish between variations in export prices due to such raw material price changes and those which are due to factors internal to the United Kingdom. It would also be useful in many contexts to have a measure of the terms of trade which compared the price of only the United Kingdom element in exports with import prices.

The price of the domestic content of exports cannot be measured directly, nor could such price information be obtained by collecting statistical returns from exporters. It can only be derived by statistical analysis, using estimates of the import content of exports to eliminate from export

---

[1] Using the ratio of import to export prices.

price changes that part which can be imputed to a change in import prices.

If we know the import content of exports and the price change of such imports, we can calculate by how much export prices should change merely because of changes in the prices of the imported materials used in exports. If we then subtract this from the actual export price change, we are left with the change in the price of the domestic content of exports.

Such a calculation clearly raises formidable statistical problems. There is first the conceptual difficulty of what is meant by the import content of exports; whether this is to be interpreted in the marginal or average sense.[1] I have used the average assumption, that is the assumption that imports of raw materials should be averaged over the whole of production, so making the import content of total production and of exports of any commodity exactly the same.

The input-output table in the Blue Book on National Income and Expenditure gives sufficient information for an estimate of the import content in 1950 of four broad categories of manufactured goods: metals, engineering and vehicles; textiles, leather and clothing; food, drink and tobacco; and other manufacturing. If we then assume that the import content of each of these groups is the same for home production and exports, we can apply these percentages to work out the average import content of exports of manufacturers[2] as a whole in 1950.

This calculation gives a figure of 18 per cent as the import content of exports of manufactures in 1950.[3] Calculations cannot be made on this basis for years other than 1950. But if we assume that, apart from the effect of price changes, the import content of exports for the four main categories does not alter over short periods, we can use the percentages obtained for 1950 to work out the average import content for other years. If we now make the further drastic assumption that the raw material average value index for all imports is also appropriate as a measure of the average price change of

[1] See W. Z. Billewicz: 'The Import Content of British Exports,' *Economica*, May 1953.

[2] The calculation has been done only for exports of manufactures, since the import content of other exports is trivial.

[3] The import content is high for textiles, leather and clothing (31 per cent) and low for metals, engineering and vehicles (11 per cent).

raw materials used in exports, we can work out year by year the increase in export prices which is merely due to such price changes. And finally we can calculate by subtraction the residual, i.e. the price change in the domestic content of exports.

The results of a calculation along these lines are given in Table III. The movement of the index of the average value of the domestic content of exports differs substantially from the total average value of exports, in any period when there is a big change in raw material prices. Thus between 1949 and 1951 when raw material import prices increased by 80 per cent, the total average value of manufactures exported increased by 20 per cent, but the average value of the domestic content of these exports by only 6 per cent. It is also worth noting that in 1953 when the average value of exports had begun to fall, the price of the domestic content of exports was still rising. We may thus easily get a false impression of the impact of changing domestic prices and costs on export prices if we merely look at total average value indices.

We also get a different picture of fluctuations in the terms of trade, if we compare the price of the domestic content of exports with import prices. The rise between 1948 and 1951 was 40 per cent, compared with the official index of only 21 per cent. Between 1951 and 1953, while import prices were falling, the domestic content price rose more steeply, and by the latter year the terms of trade on the two bases were little different compared with 1948, one showing an increase of 1 per cent and the other of 5 per cent.

This calculation involves the most hazardous assumptions and little importance should be attached to the final result. It does, however, serve to support the argument that total export average value indices conceal some of the most important changes that are taking place.

The same argument can be illustrated with greater statistical reliability from calculations of the movement of the price of the domestic content of exports of cotton goods. In working out the average import content in this case there is no problem of choosing between the marginal and average assumption, since the raw material used—raw cotton—is all imported. And it is probably safe to assume that the raw cotton content of goods sold overseas is, on average, the same as that in supplies to the home market. Using these assumptions, one can work out from the 1948 Census of Production the average raw cotton import content of exported cotton goods. This is then used in the same way as in the case of total trade to calculate that part of the fluctuation in the export average value index for cotton goods which is due to price changes of the imported materials, and so to arrive by subtraction at an index of the export price of the domestic content.

The picture revealed by these estimates (Table IV) is much more striking than for manufactures in total. Between 1950 and 1951 the average value of raw cotton imports rose from 126 to 203 (1948 = 100), but the average value of exports of cotton goods only rose from 110 to 140. This rise was barely sufficient to cover the raw material price rise, and the residual domestic content price in 1951 was little higher than in 1950 and slightly below the level of 1949. After 1951 raw material prices fell steeply but the domestic content price rose steadily, and the total average value index for cotton goods exported was the result of the combination of those two movements in opposite directions.

In these calculations of the price movements of the domestic contents of exports, changes in the average value index of imports of raw materials are related to export average values for the same period of time. This means that the change in the import content of exports is deducted in terms of its current import replacement cost, not its original cost. A substantial part of the short-period difference between the total average value and the domestic content average value may therefore be due to the fact that in practice manufacturers and exporters base their prices on the original cost of the raw materials used. For if prices are normally based on the original cost of materials, then even if there is no change in the domestic margin, the domestic content calculated on the basis used here would always show a fall for a time when import prices rise steeply, and a rise when import prices fall.

Pricing on the basis of original cost of materials is without doubt an important contributory factor explaining the movement of export prices. When import prices rise steeply, as in 1951, for a time we sell the raw material content of our exports at much lower prices than they cost us to replace. As long as exports are priced in this way we must expect the terms of trade to move against us in periods of rising raw material prices, and to move in our favour in periods of falling prices. This point can be most clearly illustrated from short period comparisons of the average value of raw cotton imports and of cotton goods exports. The average value of raw cotton imports rose steeply from 184 (1947 = 100) in the third quarter of 1950 to 355 in the second quarter of 1951, and then fell to 258 in the fourth quarter of that year. But there was practically no increase in the average value of cotton goods exported until the beginning of 1951, then a substantial increase throughout that year; and no fall until the third quarter of 1952, nearly a year after raw cotton prices had begun to fall from their peak.

The Factoral Terms of Trade

Quite a different significance is to be attached to a movement in the commodity terms of trade which results from changes in efficiency in producing goods for export, from that which reflects a change in demand. Thus when we argue that we should be able to reduce our export prices through improved efficiency and productivity, we imply that if we are successful the commodity terms of trade will turn against this country. It is important therefore, to measure how far movements in the commodity terms of trade are reinforced or offset by changes in efficiency and productivity.

We can do this by measuring changes in the factorial terms of trade. If during any period import prices increase by 20 per cent and export prices by 10 per cent, then the commodity terms of trade have increased over the period by 9 per cent; it would take an increase of 9 per cent in the volume of exports to pay for the same volume of imports as at the beginning of the period. If productivity in making goods for export over the period improves by 9 per cent, the increased volume of exports could be achieved with the same volume of factors of production. The factorial terms of trade[1] would remain unchanged, the rise in the commodity terms of trade being just offset by the increase in productivity in pro-

---

[1] This is strictly the single factorial terms of trade, the change in the volume of imports that can be bought with a unit of factors of production. The double factorial terms of trade would measure the change in the command of factors of production in the United Kingdom over factors of production overseas.

K

ducing goods for export. We can measure the factorial terms of trade, therefore, by dividing the index of the commodity terms of trade by an index of the productivity of factors producing goods for export.

Such a calculation raises many conceptual and practical problems, none of which can be solved satisfactorily at present. The following explanation of the method used to arrive at the figures in Table V is put forward as illustrating these problems, and, as with most of the other figures in this article, no great reliance should be placed on the final result.

Apart from the difficulty of defining what is meant by a 'unit of factors of production', there is at present no way of measuring changes in the productivity of factors other than labour. The main basis for any general measurement of changes in labour productivity must be a comparison of the movement of the volume of production and employment. The official index of industrial production is available in detail back to 1946, and there is a comparison between 1935 and 1946 for broad industrial groupings. But there is no continuous series of employment figures for this period, and the only way of arriving at indices of employment is to link together three different sets of statistics.[1]

Since we are interested in changes in productivity of manufacture for export, the grouping of the production and employment series has to be arranged to correspond with that used in the export statistics. This can only be done if eleven[2] broad categories are used, and of these eleven, five— chemicals; metal manufacture; engineering; vehicles; and textiles—now account for over 80 per cent of total exports. Indices of output per head for 1935 and 1946 to 1953 were worked out for each of the eleven groups. They were then combined to give a total productivity index, using the distribution of export trade in 1948 as weights. Alternative weights were also tried: the 1935 distribution of trade in making the comparison with pre-war, and the 1953 distribu-

---

[1] The two sets of Ministry of Labour figures, before and after June 1948 for the years 1946–1953, and the Census of Production figures of employment for 1935 and 1949.

[2] Food, drink and tobacco; chemical and allied trades; metal manufacture; vehicles (excluding ships); engineering and electrical goods, instruments and ships; textiles; clothing; manufactures of wood and cork; paper and printing; leather goods; and miscellaneous manufactures.

tion of trade in making comparisons for years since 1948.

This method of calculation implies the assumption that in each broad group the change in output per head for goods exported was the same as for total production. Some of the results of the calculation, especially in the comparison with 1935, give quite startling results. Output per head in vehicles production, for example, comes out as very much lower in the whole post-war period than in 1935.[1] Indeed the results mainly serve to raise doubts and suspicions about the reliability of existing production and employment indices comparing the pre-war and post-war periods. A more detailed and reliable comparison could perhaps be made for 1935 and 1948 from the Census of Production Reports for those two years, but no estimates of changes in the volume of production calculated from the material in the Census have yet been published.

Less doubt attaches to the significance of the results from 1948 onwards since the basic statistics are much more reliable for that period. The export productivity index shows a rise of 15 per cent between 1948 and 1953. Since the commodity terms of trade increased by 1 per cent over the same period, this gives a figure of 88 per cent for the factorial terms of trade in 1953 compared with 1948 (100). Assuming a continuation of the same average rate of increase in productivity as over the last five years, implies that the factorial terms of trade will continue to improve as long as the commodity terms of trade do not on average deteriorate by more than about $2\frac{1}{2}$ per cent per annum.

These figures measure the factorial terms of trade for merchandise trade only. Measures of productivity for invisible items exported would be needed to calculate the factorial terms for trade as a whole, but there is no basis for arriving at such measures.

The Income Terms of Trade

All these figures direct attention to the relative movement of import and export prices and pay no regard to the effects of such price movements on the volume of imports or exports. We know that a favourable movement in the terms of trade

[1] Even in 1953, 18 per cent or 26 per cent (according to whether 1935 or 1946 weights are used in the comparison between those two years) below 1935.

measured in this way may be favourable only in a technical
sense. If, for example, internal costs and export prices of this
country increase while those of our competitors and suppliers
remain unchanged, the volume of exports from this country
might fall severely and the balance of payments problem be
substantially aggravated; yet the terms of trade would move
in our favour.

In interpreting the significance of a movement in the
terms of trade one must therefore pay regard to the effect of
price movements on the volume of trade. Mr Dorrance has
suggested that a convenient way of doing this statistically is
to measure changes in the import purchasing power of exports
and he calls this measure 'the income terms of trade'.[1] The
income terms of trade are calculated simply by dividing an
index of the value of exports by an index of the price of
imports. It thus takes account of three factors: the quantity
of goods exported, changes in the average value of exports,
and changes in the average value of imports. The final index
measures the changing volume of imports that could be
bought with the income obtained from exports. The index
reflects not only the relative movement of import and export
prices and the effect of such movements on the volume of
exports, but all the other factors which influence the export
trade of the country. If there are no items in foreign transactions other than merchandise imports and exports, the income
terms of trade will, of course, be the same as an index of the
volume of actual imports.

The income terms of trade can be calculated either for
merchandise trade alone, or where the information is available
for invisible items of trade as well. Both sets of figures are
given in Table VI. It will be seen that there is very little
difference between the two sets of figures, except in comparison with pre-war,[2] but a distinct difference between these
movements and those shown by the other measures of the
terms of trade, not only in magnitude but frequently in
direction. Between 1949 and 1950, for example, when the
commodity terms of trade deteriorated by 7 per cent, the

---

[1] See G. S. Dorrance: The Income Terms of Trade, *The Review of Economic
Studies* 1948–1949. Vol. XVI, pp. 50–56.

[2] This reflects the relative decline in income from invisible items compared
with pre-war.

increase in the volume of exports was sufficient to improve the income terms of trade by 8 per cent. Thus the income terms of trade provides a useful supplementary index of the changing foreign trade position of a country.

Sectional Import and Export Price Indices
So far discussion has been largely confined to indices which measure the average price of imports and exports as a whole. In the last few years there have been wide differences in price movement within each of these averages, and concentration on the average figures results in significant and interesting changes being ignored.

There has been a striking difference between the movement of the prices of imports of food and raw materials. Raw materials have been responsible for the major increases and fluctuations in import prices since 1947, while food prices have remained relatively stable. Between 1947 and 1951 food import prices increased by 37 per cent, while raw material prices increased by 116 per cent. Since that year raw material prices have fallen steeply although in 1953 they were still 64 per cent higher than in 1947; but food import prices have hardly changed since 1951 (Table VII).

There is a remarkably close similarity since 1946 between the movement of food import prices and the movement in prices of exports of manufactured goods. Indeed the whole of the adverse trend and fluctuation in the terms of trade over the period is due to changes in the relation between raw material import prices and export prices of manufactured goods; none to any change in the relation of the prices of food imported and manufactures exported. This can be seen quite clearly from the two subsidiary terms of trade indices given in Table VII; the first showing the ratio of the price of food imports to the price of manufactures exported, the second the ratio of the price of raw materials imported to the price of manufactures exported. The food/manufactures terms of trade shows relatively little change since 1946, only varying from 98 to 103. The raw materials/manufactures index rises slowly at first, from 83 in 1946 to 100 in 1949, then sharply to 148 in 1951, and has since fallen back to 107 in 1953. It is undoubtedly the terms on which we exchange raw materials for manufactures which has been the determining factor in fluctuations in the terms of trade since 1946; changes in the demand and supply of food have had only a minor influence.

There is also a striking range of variation in the price movement of different categories of manufactures exported (Table VIII). There are two fairly clearly defined classes. Those where imported raw materials are of importance, such as textiles, paper and cardboard and non-ferrous metals; and those where the raw material content is small or mainly home produced, such as iron and steel manufactures, electrical goods, machinery, chemicals and vehicles. The prices of exports in the first group rise with rising prices of imported materials but only after a considerable time lag, suggesting as was argued earlier, that prices are fixed in terms of original rather than replacement cost of raw materials. In the second group domestic costs appear to be the determining element in prices. The average value of exports of manufactures of chemicals, iron and steel manufactures and machinery were remarkably stable throughout 1949 and 1950. It was not until the second quarter of 1951, nearly twelve months after the beginning of the Korean boom, that export prices of these goods began to rise and then only slowly. But prices went on rising throughout 1952 and most of 1953 when prices of exports in the first category had been falling for some time.

The main explanation of fluctuations in prices of exports must be sought in movements in costs, and there is little evidence that changing demand or competitive conditions in overseas markets exerts much direct influence. Any narrowing or widening of profit margins as overseas trading conditions change has singularly little effect on prices. If this interpretation of the export figures is correct, it suggests that the fluctuations in the United Kingdom's terms of trade since 1946 have been due much more to the difference between the market structure determining prices of raw materials and manufactures, than to any serious divergence between the underlying demand and supply conditions for the two sets of commodities.

TABLE I
MERCHANDISE TERMS OF TRADE
1948 = 100

	Imports (Average Value)	Exports (Average Value)	Terms of Trade Imports / Exports
1938[1]	35	41	85
1945[1]	69	76	91
1946[2]	74	81	91
1947[2]	90	92	98
1948[2]	100	100	100
1949[2]	102	103	99
1950[2]	115	108	106
1951[2]	150	125	121
1952[3]	149	134	111
1953[3]	132	130	101

[1] Original indices based on 1938=100.
[2] Original indices based on 1947=100.
[3] Original indices based on 1950=100.

TABLE II
ALL FOREIGN TRANSACTIONS[1]: TERMS OF TRADE
1948 = 100

	Imports (Average Value)	Exports (Average Value)	Terms of Trade Imports / Exports
1946	81	84	96
1947	93	92	101
1948	100	100	100
1949	102	103	99
1950	118	109	109
1951	149	128	117
1952	144	133	109

[1] All items in the current account of the Balance of Payments excluding interest, dividends and profits.

TABLE III
'DOMESTIC CONTENT' MERCHANDISE TERMS OF TRADE
1948 = 100

	Imports[1] (Average Value)	Domestic Content of Exports (Average Value)	Terms of Trade Imports / Domestic Content of Exports
1945	69	79	87
1946	74	81	91
1947	90	95	95
1948	100	100	100
1949	102	101	101
1950	115	102	113
1951	150	107	140
1952	149	123	121
1953	132	126	105

[1] As in Table I.

TABLE IV

PRICE OF IMPORTS OF RAW COTTON
and
EXPORTS OF COTTON MANUFACTURES
1948 = 100

	Raw Cotton Imports (Average Value)	Cotton Manufactures Exports (Average Value)	Raw Cotton Import Price effect on Cotton Manufactures Exports[4] (Average Value)	Cotton Manufactures Exports: Domestic Content (Average Value)
1946[1]	47	70	81	83
1947[1]	64	85	87	97
1948[1]	100	100	100	100
1949[1]	97	103	99	106
1950[2]	126	111	109	103
1951[2]	203	139	136	105
1952[3]	171	133	125	112
1953[3]	115	115	105	115

[1] Original indices based on 1938 = 100.
[2] Original indices based on 1947 = 100.
[3] Original indices based on 1950 = 100.
[4] Index of the average value of exports of cotton manufactures if there had been no change in price except that due to changes in prices of raw cotton.

TABLE V

FACTORIAL TERMS OF TRADE
1948 = 100

	Merchandise Terms of Trade[1]	Output per head in Production of Exports	Factorial Terms of Trade
1935 (a)[2]	84	100[4]—103[5]	84—82
(b)[3]		103[4]—105[5]	82—80
1946	91	93	98
1947	98	94	104
1948	100	100	100
1949	99	105	94
1950	106	107	99
1951	121	112	108
1952	111	108	103
1953	101	115[5]—116[6]	88—87

[1] As in Table I.
[2] Using 1935 net outputs in weighting 1935 and 1946.
[3] Using 1946 net outputs in weighting 1935 and 1946.
[4] Using 1938 distribution of exports to combine indices of productivity for individual industrial groups.
[5] Using 1948 distribution of exports to combine indices of productivity for individual industrial groups.
[6] Using 1953 distribution of exports to combine indices of productivity for individual industrial groups.

Table VI

INCOME TERMS OF TRADE
1948 = 100

| | Total Export Income | Price of all Imports (Average Value)[1] | Merchandise Exports Income | Price of Merchandise Imports (Average Value)[2] | Income Terms of Trade | |
					Total Trade	Merchandise Trade
1938	40	38[3]	32	35	105	91
1946	66	81	59	74	81	78
1947	75	93	73	90	81	81
1948	100	100	100	100	100	100
1949	110	102	112	102	108	110
1950	138	118	137	115	117	119
1951	165	149	164	150	111	109
1952	167	144	164	149	116	110
1953	160	—	163	132	—	123

[1] As in Table 2.
[2] As in Table I.
[3] Assuming the price change of all imports between 1938 and 1946 the same as the price change for merchandise imports.

Table VII

FOOD/MANUFACTURES AND RAW MATERIALS/ MANUFACTURES TERMS OF TRADE
1948 = 100

| | Exports of Manufactures (Average Value) | Food Imports (Average Value) | Raw Materials Imports (Average Value) | Terms of Trade | |
				Food Imports / Exports of Manufactures	Raw Materials Imports / Exports of Manufactures
1938	41	36	31	88	76
1945	77	67	65	87	84
1946	81	80	67	99	83
1947	92	93	85	101	92
1948	100	100	100	100	100
1949	103	102	103	99	100
1950	107	110	125	103	117
1951	124	127	183	102	148
1952	134	132	170	99	127
1953	130	127	139	98	107

TABLE VIII

PRICES (AVERAGE VALUE) OF EXPORTS OF MANUFACTURES BY MAIN GROUPS

1948 = 100

	Total Manufactures	Cotton Goods	Woollen Goods	Non-Ferrous Metal Manfcts.	Paper and Cardboard	Iron and Steel	Electrical Goods	Machinery	Vehicles	Chemicals
1949[1]	101	103	105	105	100	104	102	103	104	101
1950 1st Qr.[2]	103	105	109	117	94	105	103	106	106	101
2nd Qr.[2]	104	109	118	124	93	104	105	107	105	101
3rd Qr.[2]	106	111	124	135	98	103	103	108	107	102
4th Qr.[2]	108	116	136	142	105	102	105	109	108	100
1951 1st Qr.[2]	114	125	153	153	119	108	111	111	113	96
2nd Qr.[2]	119	135	179	163	137	115	116	115	119	100
3rd Qr.[2]	125	146	190	166	160	123	122	118	125	107
4th Qr.[2]	128	152	181	165	163	132	125	121	128	109
1952 1st Qr.[2]	131	148	169	177	171	137	129	125	131	119
2nd Qr.[2]	132	142	149	181	170	146	133	130	133	120
3rd Qr.[3]	130	126	139	181	163	149	133	133	135	118
4th Qr.[3]	128	119	136	176	149	150	133	136	134	107
1953 1st Qr.[3]	128	117	139	180	142	151	133	137	131	108
2nd Qr.[3]	126	114	145	170	139	148	129	139	129	104
3rd Qr.[3]	125	111	150	156	133	145	130	142	129	102
4th Qr.[3]	126	114	151	158	133	143	125	142	130	102

[1] Originally based on 1938 = 100.
[2] Originally based on 1947 = 100.
[3] Originally based on 1950 = 100.

The Wage-Price Spiral[1]

I

THE simple view of the wage-price spiral is that wages go up in an attempt to offset price increases; that such wage increases put up costs; that industry meets these by putting up prices; and that with this increase in prices there is pressure for further wage increases. As each round is completed the stage is set for the next upward twist in the spiral. This view, although it contains the essential spiral element of the phenomenon, oversimplifies the interrelation between wages, costs and prices. This interrelation is highly complex and intricate, being influenced by many factors. Of these, movements in import prices, indirect taxation and subsidies, controls, productivity, profit and distributive margins are of great importance. To disentangle the connection between these and the main movements in wages and retail prices in this country in recent years would be a major research task for which the statistical information is in many ways inadequate. All that will be attempted here is the less ambitious task of throwing some light on what has in fact been happening, if merely to show how misleading it is to think in terms of the simple wages, costs, prices picture.

II

In May 1956 the level of retail prices, as measured by the retail price index number, was 57 per cent higher than in June 1947.[2] The different movement of the price of the main categories of goods and services included in the indexes is very striking. Compared with the average increase of 57 per cent, food had increased by 96 per cent, fuel and light by 75 per cent, services by 51 per cent, clothing, house-

[1] *District Bank Review*, September 1956.
[2] The comparison is made with June 1947 not because this date has any special economic significance, but because this is when the present series of price index numbers starts.

hold durable goods and miscellaneous goods by between 42–9 per cent, rent and rates by 26 per cent, and drink and tobacco by only 15 per cent. Equally striking is the fact that this pattern of price increases has not persisted throughout the period but has changed a great deal from time to time. It would be tedious to trace this changing pattern in its full detail but the following facts are both important and enlightening.

1. The prices of those goods made by manufacturing industry—clothing, household durable goods and miscellaneous goods—have moved very differently, especially in timing, from the rest of the items. There was a slow upward rise in the early years, a very sharp upward twist in the second half of 1950 and 1951, and then three years, 1952, 1953 and 1954, of stable or even falling prices. At the end of 1954 the index numbers for these three groups were 141, 130 and 137 compared with 147, 136 and 137 at the end of 1951. Yet the over-all index was rising throughout these years, indicating a very different movement in some of the other items. From the beginning of 1955 there has been a resumption of a slow upward rise in the three groups.

2. Food prices have been rising throughout the whole period, but the periods of steepest increase were in 1949, 1951 and 1952 and since the beginning of 1954.

3. Fuel and light and services have risen steadily throughout the period.

4. Rent and rates remained practically unchanged from 1947 to 1952, and since then have risen slowly but continuously.

5. After an increase in the early years, alcohol and tobacco prices have remained practically unchanged.

Clearly these divergent movements cannot be explained in any simple way by relative movements in wage rates. Unfortunately the Ministry of Labour's index of wage rates gives figures only for the average of industry as a whole, but there is sufficient evidence to support the view that there have not been great differences between different industries and services. Certainly the figures of movements in the average level of earnings, in so far as they are available, support this view, although earnings have over this period been affected by other influences apart from changes in rates. One must look elsewhere if one is to explain such large divergences.

III

The peculiar movement of two sections—rent and rates, and alcohol and tobacco—can be explained quite simply. The element of indirect tax in the price of alcohol and tobacco is so great that any movement in production cost, manufacturers' price, and distributive margins have an insignificant proportionate effect on the final retail price. The relative stability of prices over the last few years reflects merely the substantially unchanged, although very high, level of indirect taxation on these items.

The movement of the rent and rates index—the stability in the early years, and the slow, continuous rise since 1952—is partly a reflection of the change in the way the index has been calculated. Up till 1952 only pre-war working-class houses were included in the index, and, being subject to control, the rent of these was virtually unchanged. Since 1952 post-war local authority housing has been included, and the rise largely reflects the increase in these rents and the slow rise in rates.

It is important to remember that while these two sections—tobacco and drink, and housing—reflect changing levels of indirect taxation and rates, no account is of course taken in the measurement of prices of changes in the level of direct taxation, such as PAYE. Whether workers and Trade Unions are affected in their attitudes and policies more by changes in indirect taxes which show themselves directly in prices, than by direct taxation such as PAYE which affects money incomes, is an interesting question, but very difficult to answer.

IV

The main interest lies, therefore, in the divergent movement in prices of manufactured goods, fuel and light and services, and food. An analysis of the factors affecting prices of manufactured goods is particularly interesting since these prices are of major importance in our export trade as well as in affecting the working of our economy at home. Here indirect taxation, in the form of purchase tax, although of importance has played a minor role. This can be seen from the striking similarity of the movement in wholesale prices of manufactures, export prices of manufactures, and retail prices of those goods produced by manufacturing industry. All show the same marked rise in 1950 and 1951, stability or a gradual fall in 1952, 1953 and 1954, and a slow upward movement since the beginning of 1955. This movement is a compound effect of changes in raw material, especially imported raw material, costs, wage rates and other internal costs, and productivity. Although it is not possible to measure accurately the contribution that each of these has made to final prices, there is sufficient evidence to form some picture of the changing role played by each.

Prices of imported raw materials rose very steeply in 1950 and 1951 (the average level of prices of imports of basic materials was over 60 per cent higher in 1951 than in 1950), partly as the result of the devaluation of 1949, and partly because of the international boom in raw materials after the outbreak of the Korean war. Prices then fell steeply in 1952, and remained stable at the new lower level in 1953 and 1954. In 1955 there was a slight upward movement, but even now (mid-1956) prices are barely higher than the level of 1953 and much lower than in 1951 or 1952. There have, of course, been differences in movement within the average— for example between cotton, wool and non-ferrous metals— but in general British industry has had the benefit of either falling or relatively stable raw material import prices since 1952. Costs of some home materials used by manufacturing industry have moved very differently, the outstanding case being coal, which has risen steadily in price year by year. This has also had a major effect on the pattern of prices of home raw materials, such as steel and cement, where fuel is an important item of cost. But if fuel is excluded, one gets a similar pattern of raw material costs even when home materials are included. The Board of Trade's wholesale price index of materials (excluding fuel) used in non-food manufacturing industry, reached 193 on average in 1951 (June 1949 = 100), fell to 162 in 1952, and 146 in 1953. After a period of stability it began to rise again towards the end of 1954 and now (June 1956 stands) at 155.

Throughout the whole period wages have been rising, although at varying rates. In October 1955 average earnings in manufacturing industries were 60 per cent higher than in mid-1948. But productivity, as measured by output per man employed, has also been rising over this period. For manufacturing as a whole output per man employed rose by 25 per cent between 1948 and 1955. The rise was interrupted during the recession in production in 1952, and has been reversed again during recent months. In other years it has varied from 2–6 per cent. In the period 1952–4, the rise in productivity coupled with falling or stable material prices was sufficient to offset the rise in money wage rates, and final prices of manufactured goods were therefore kept relatively stable. At the beginning of 1955 raw material prices began to rise again, the rise in money earnings in manufacturing industries has been greater than the rise in productivity, and there has been an appreciable and steady rise in wholesale and retail prices of manufactures.

The relative importance of movements of raw material prices, money wage rates and productivity, has, of course, differed from industry to industry. Productivity has risen most in chemicals (52 per cent above 1948 in 1955), and least in textiles (11 per cent) and clothing (13 per cent). There have been intermediate rises in vehicles (35 per cent), metals (24 per cent) and engineering (30 per cent). But although the increase in productivity in textiles and clothing has been small and the rise in money earnings not much less than the average, clothing and textiles prices, both at the wholesale and retail level, have tended to fall slightly over the last three or four years. This is because of the rapid fall in raw material prices from the peak Korean boom levels of 1951, a fall which has been more than sufficient to offset rises in other costs over the period.

Iron and steel is another interesting example of the varying effects of prices of imported materials, costs of home materials, wage rates and productivity. During 1951 and early 1952, under the impact of rising imported material costs, rising wage rates and rising fuel prices, final steel prices rose by nearly 40 per cent. In the next three years the price of coal and wage rates in steel continued to rise, but the fall in the price of imported materials and the rise in productivity in steel production were sufficient to offset these. From February 1952 to July 1955, the general level of steel prices in this country remained virtually unchanged. But in 1955 prices of imported materials began to rise again, and since then import prices have tended to reinforce, rather than to offset, the rise in costs due to rising coal prices and wage rates. Prices were put up in July 1955 and June 1956, and are now (July) rather more than 10 per cent higher than in the beginning of 1955.

The year 1955 was thus a crucial one for prices, both home and export, of British manufactures, In 1952, 1953 and 1954, in general the rise in productivity coupled with the fall in imported raw material costs was sufficient to offset almost completely the increases in wage rates and earnings, so that prices, wholesale, export and retail, were either stable or falling. In 1955 prices of imported raw materials began to rise again, productivity increased rather less than in 1953 and 1954, while money wage earnings increased rather more. All forces combined therefore towards pushing up prices of manufactures. In June 1956 wholesale prices of manufactures (other than fuel and food) were 6 per cent higher than a year earlier, export prices were up 4 per cent (metals 8 per cent, engineering products 4 per cent and textiles unchanged), and retail prices of the main group of goods produced by British manufacturing industry were up from 4–9 per cent. Some of this increase at the retail level, is, however, a reflection of the increased rates of purchase tax imposed last Autumn.

This brief analysis of recent changes in the prices of manufactures pays no attention to changes in costs apart from raw materials and wages, or to variations in profit margins. There is a current fashion in academic economics to treat profit margins as a fixed proportionate addition to cost. There is indeed evidence that prices of most manufactures do not fluctuate freely with the changing pressure of demand, and that they are substantially determined by costs. But there may still be some room for variation in profit margins. It would indeed by difficult to account for the relative stability of prices of British exports of some manufactured products, especially engineering goods, in the last nine months in face of rising raw material prices and increases in wages in excess of productivity increases, unless profit margins have narrowed.

v

The steady upward movement of prices of the fuel and light group is fairly easy to explain. The price of coal is

determined by miners' wages. Average wage earnings in
coal mining in 1955 were 60 per cent higher than in 1948.
By contrast with manufacturing, output per man employed in
mining and quarrying was barely 10 per cent higher in 1955
than in 1948 and the whole of this increase took place by
1951, since when there has been no increase at all. Consequently the price of fuel used in manufacturing industry,
as well as at retail, has risen steadily. Indeed since imported
raw materials play little role in its production and productivity
remains depressingly stable, coal seems to be the one case
where there is a simple, direct relation between the movements of wage rates and prices.

The factors affecting the prices of services included in the
final index of retail prices are more difficult to disentangle.
The main items included, until the most recent revisions in
the index, were travel, postage and entertainment. All these
services have been affected by rises in costs which cannot be
substantially offset by changes in productivity. Increases in
wage rates for workers in these industries in line with increases in the rest of industry, inevitably mean a gradually rising price level for services. It is true that the rise in
prices may be moderated for a time in those service industries
where there is a heavy element of capital equipment, as
allowance may not be made for this on a replacement basis.
But, in general, the prices of services will only rise less than
the prices of manufactured goods when the latter are being
pushed up by increases in raw material import prices. When
raw material import prices are stable or falling, prices of
services are almost certain to go up relatively to manufactures. Thus during the period 1952-4 when retail prices
of manufactures were stable, the price index for services rose
by 13 per cent.

Where there are disparate rises in productivity in different
sectors of the economy, the application of the view that
increases in productivity warrant increases in wages, is itself bound to mean a gradually rising general price level.
If increases in productivity occur mainly in manufacturing,
as they have done in recent years and are likely to continue
to do, then increases in wages in manufacturing in line with
increases in productivity would, apart from changes in
import prices, make possible a stable price level for manu-

L

factured goods. But the force of competition in the labour market as well as Trade Union bargaining would drive up wages elsewhere, in services and mining, to keep in step with movements in manufacturing; and since productivity is hardly increasing at all in these industries, prices would rise with the rise in wage rates. In these circumstances, therefore, prices of manufactured products would remain stable, but the prices of other goods and services would rise steadily, thus giving an over-all upward moving price level. The only way to have an over-all stable price level would be for wages in manufacturing to rise substantially less than productivity and for the price level in manufacturing to fall sufficiently to offset the rise in the prices of other goods and services. To suggest a rise of wage rates in manufacturing less than the rise in productivity is perhaps asking the impossible; but it is important to realize that a stable level of costs in manufacturing industry and of prices of manufactured products, by no means guarantees a stable level of over-all prices.

VI

The movement of food prices is of special importance in its contribution to the movement of prices facing the final consumer. In the new retail price index food accounts for 35 per cent of total expenditure, and in the earlier index which it replaced, the weight attached to food was higher still at 40 per cent. These figures are for working-class expenditure to which the index of retail prices largely relates. But even for consumers' expenditure as a whole the proportion going to food was as high as 32 per cent in 1954.

The movement of food prices is also of importance, because it was mainly the substantial rise in retail food prices in 1954 and 1955 which made the general movement of retail prices in this country so different from that in most other industrial countries. As measured by the retail price index, food prices in this country rose by 8 per cent in 1954 and 5 per cent in 1955. By contrast during this period retail food prices in the United States and Canada fell slightly; indeed in both countries retail food prices had been falling steadily since 1952. In Belgium, France, Holland and Austria food prices were practically unchanged over the years 1954 and

1955; in Germany, Italy and Norway prices rose over the
two years by 5 per cent; and in Switzerland by 3 per cent.
Only Sweden (10 per cent) and Denmark (14 per cent) had
increases comparable with the United Kingdom. It was this
difference in the movement of food prices which largely
accounted for the contrast between a steadily rising retail
price level in the United Kingdom and relatively stable retail prices in most of the rest of Europe and N. America.

It is particularly difficult to disentangle quantitatively the
various factors which have contributed to the rise in retail
food prices in this country over the last three or four years.
For during this period there have been big shifts in consumption and changes in quality, as well as the gradual decontrol
of food marketing, the reduction of food subsidies, and
variations in import prices and costs in home agriculture.
Apart from the difficult theoretical problems involved in
trying to disentangle separately the effect of each of these,
there is at present not enough published statistical information
to do this. All one can do is to review in turn those factors
on which there are a few figures. In view of the major role
that food prices play in the movements of the retail price
index (three-quarters of the rise in the retail price index
in 1955 compared with 1954 was due to increased food
prices), it is surprising how little published information
there is on the factors influencing the changing price of food.

First of all it is important to realise that the rise in the price
of food shown in the official retail price index is appreciably
greater than the rise in price of consumers' food expenditure
as a whole. On the basis of the retail price indexes food prices
in the first quarter of 1956 were 75 per cent higher than in
1948; the comparable figure for the price of the food section
of general consumers' expenditure was 63 per cent. Part of
the difference may be due to the different methods of calculation used. The comparison also suggests that it is the
food items particularly prominent in working class expenditure which have risen most in price. But although there is a
margin of difference between the two indexes, both, of
course, show a substantial rise in food prices in recent years.

Food import prices rose steeply in the years immediately
before 1952, although not as much as raw material prices.
In the year 1952 food import prices were about 55 per cent

higher than in 1947,[1] and a substantial part of the rise in retail food prices over this period can be attributed to the rising cost of food imports. But in later years import prices have been stable or falling; in 1955 they were only 52 per cent above 1947. Even in recent months, by contrast with raw materials, there has been little sign of any rise in import prices.

Since 1948–9 there has been a substantial fall in the level of food and agricultural subsidies from £484 million in that year to £239 million in 1954–5. Indeed had the sum of money devoted to subsidies remained unchanged over the period the proportionate effect on prices would have been much reduced. The volume of food consumption has been increasing steadily in recent years and the subsidies would therefore, in any case, have been spread over a larger expenditure, and consequently had a smaller effect in reducing prices. In addition, as the general level of food prices rose even the same absolute figure of food subsidies would have had a progressively reduced proportionate effect on prices.

In 1955 consumers' total expenditure on food was over 80 per cent higher in money terms than in 1948, and 16 per cent higher after allowing for price changes. This increase in the volume of food consumption, the increase in the general level of prices, and the reduction in the food subsidies, have meant a very drastic reduction in the proportionate effect of food subsidies on prices. As a percentage of total consumers' expenditure on food, subsidies fell from 21 per cent in 1948–9 to 14 per cent in 1951–2 and 6 per cent in 1954–5. These figures refer to all consumers' expenditure and since the subsidies were particularly concentrated on basic food items, a similar calculation for wage-earners' expenditure alone, if it could be done, would probably show an even greater fall.

Decontrol has also had a substantial effect in the last few years. There has been a shift in patterns of consumption, a wider range of choice, and probably in some cases, for example meat, a switch to higher qualities. How far the increase in prices is a reflection of these factors it is difficult to tell. There is also some evidence that distributive margins on some

---

[1] I am indebted to Mr Thomas and Miss Walker of the Agricultural Economics Department at Manchester University for these figures and others given in the following paragraphs.

commodities have increased since decontrol and have contributed to the rise in food prices. These increased margins may represent the costs of better service and the wider range of choice available, but also a higher rate of profit under the pressure of increased demand in the last two or three prosperous years. A preliminary but rather crude attempt at measuring the distributive margin for meat, for example, shows a margin in 1954 over 50 per cent greater than in 1950. Distributive margins for milk have also increased appreciably since 1951.

This still leaves us with costs and profit margins in United Kingdom farming. There is no satisfactory published measure of these. Costs seem to have been going up appreciably although they have been absorbed to some extent by increased productivity resulting from greater mechanization and an increased use of fertilisers.

All this hardly gives a satisfactory analysis of the important elements contributing to the rise in food prices in recent years, but it is difficult to take the argument much further.

VII

The main argument of this article is that the movement of retail prices in the last few years, both overall and in its constituent elements, cannot be simply explained as part of a wage-price spiral. Changing import prices, productivity, indirect taxes and subsidies, decontrol, as well as certain peculiarities in the official statistics of retail prices, have all played an important role. And yet paradoxically the effect of wage changes on prices is likely to be more obvious and direct in coming months. As to the reasons for this, import prices, both of food and raw materials, are now relatively stable and are unlikely to offset an upward movement in internal costs; decontrol and the reduction of subsidies have a once for all effect, and even further moves in this direction would now have a much smaller proportionate effect on prices. Indeed for the time being at least the simple crude notion of the wage-price spiral may be more relevant to our situation than it has been for some time.

10

An Index of Wage-Rates by Industries[1,2]

I

THE official index of rates of wages published monthly by
the Ministry of Labour gives two series of figures, each for
men, women and juveniles; one for 'All Industries and Services', the other 'Manufacturing Industries only'. Apart from
this very broad division, no indices of wage-rates by industries
are published in this country.[3] Clearly a more detailed industrial index would be of great value for many purposes. It
would make possible, for example, a more fruitful analysis of
the structure of wage movements and of the relative movements of wage-rates and wage-earnings in the post-war
period.[4] We have tried to calculate such indices using
published information.

The indices start in 1948, are calculated on 1948 as base,
and are weighted by wage-bills in that year. 1948 was chosen

[1] The Manchester School, May 1958, jointly with R. C. Ogley.

[2] Most of our colleagues at Manchester have helped us at some stage with
the problems, both theoretical and practical, that arose in calculating this index, but we would like particularly to thank Mr H. A. F. Turner, Mrs G.
Hansell, Miss A. M. Martin and Mr J. R. Crossley. We are also much indebted to Mrs H. Collins, Miss H. Grzesiukowicz and Miss Tyrrell and previous members of the computing staff for their patience and stamina in doing
the tabulating and calculating work.

[3] The London and Cambridge Economic Service publish indices of 'Quoted
Full-Time Wage Rates,' but these cover only a limited range of occupations,
and since March 1954, they have not been used to calculate a general index of
wage-rates (See The Times Review of Industry, March 1954, London and
Cambridge Economic Service, p. viii). In 1935, Mr E. C. Ramsbottom, then
Director of Statistics at the Ministry of Labour, published indices of wage-
rates by industries for the inter-war years, but unfortunately these indices were
not continued in published form in the post-war period (See E. C. Ramsbottom, 'The Course of Wage Rates in the United Kingdom, 1921–1934,'
J. R. Statistical Society, 1935, Pt. IV, p. 639; 'Wage Rates in the United Kingdom, 1934–1937,' J. R. Statistical Society, 1938, Pt. 1, p. 202; and 'Wage Rates
in the United Kingdom in 1938, ' J. R. Statistical Society, 1939, Pt. II, p. 289).

[4] Also, once the basic material has been extracted and prepared for an
industrial index, it could be used for calculating indices by other criteria of
grouping (e.g. by degrees of skill, or by region, or by institutional form of
wage-fixing).

because of the availability of detailed earnings statistics for that year, and also because other important indices, such as the index of industrial production, are based on 1948.[1]

In this article we explain the way in which the indices are compiled, discuss some of the problems of both principle and statistical practice that arise in the calculations, and give the main results for the period 1948 to 1956. We also compare the movement of wage-rates with the movement of wage-earnings over this period. In a later article it is hoped to bring the indices up-to-date on a monthly basis, and to discuss in more detail some of the issues, statistical and economic, which are raised by the results.

II

Two publications of the Ministry of Labour are used for the basic information about rates and changes in rates; firstly the annual *Time Rates of Wages and Hours of Labour* which gives the rates of wages in effect on April 1st of the year to which the publication relates,[2] and secondly the table in each issue of the monthly *Ministry of Labour Gazette* which gives the *Principal Changes in Rates of Wages* reported during the previous month. In order to appreciate the significance of the indices which we compile from this material, it is important to understand the basis of this information published by the Ministry of Labour.

The information which the Ministry of Labour obtains and publishes on wage-rates arises from the operation of the systems of collective bargaining and of wage fixing by Statutory Authorities. The rates published are a summary of the rates agreed in these bargains, awarded by Tribunals, or fixed by Statutory authorities. Since Statutory rates are distinguished separately in *Time Rates of Wages and Hours of Labour*, it is possible to work out the relative importance of these compared with Non-Statutory rates. This information is

---

[1] The interpretation of the comparative movement of rates between different industries may be affected by the choice of this year as the basis. For one group may have been just at the head of the wage round in that year and another at the tail of a previous round. The importance of this factor will be dealt with in a later article.

[2] The dates to which the rates relate has been April 1st in publication since 1954. In 1947 and 1948 it was September, and from 1949 to 1952, October. There was no publication for 1953.

given in Table I. In the index, as a whole, Statutory rates account for 22 per cent of the total weights.[1] Statutory rates are much more important for women's rates (46 per cent of the total weights for women) than for men's (18 per cent of the weights). The industries in which Statutory rates predominate are Agriculture; Clothing; Food, Drink and Tobacco; Metal Goods n.e.s.; and Miscellaneous Services. Statutory rates are of some, but lesser, importance in Textiles; Leather; Manufacturers of Wood and Cork; Paper and Printing; Other Manufacturing; Transport, Distribution and Public Administration. In other industries (Mining; Treatment of Non-Metalliferous Mining Products; Chemicals: Metal Manufacture; Engineering, Shipbuilding and Electrical Goods; Vehicles; Precision Instruments; Building and Contracting; Gas, Electricity and Water and Professional Services) the rates used are all Non-Statutory, i.e. the results of collective bargaining.

Since the material in the Ministry of Labour's publications relates to Statutory rates or rates agreed by collective bargaining, rates in industries or occupations not covered by either of these systems are not given and are therefore not covered by our index. Statutory rates and collective bargaining between them now cover, directly or indirectly, most wage-earners. The only Order[2] not covered by any rates at all in the index is Insurance, Banking and Finance (Order XXI). Two other Orders, Professional Services (XXIII) and Miscellaneous Services (XXIV) are only partially covered. In Miscellaneous Services, for example, there are no rates for resident domestic service, which in terms of wages bill accounts for about one-quarter of the Order. There are other industries and occupations for which no rates are available, but except for the three cases mentioned above they do not account for a substantial part of an Order. A list of Minimum List Headings of the Standard Industrial Classification not covered by any rate at all, and their importance in each Order, is given in Table II.

In many agreements and wage orders separate rates are

---

[1] See pages 179–184 for an explanation of the weighting system used.

[2] The analysis and grouping of rates is done throughout on the basis of the Orders and Minimum List Headings used in the Standard Industrial Classification.

fixed for juveniles. But the rates for juveniles are not given regularly either in *Times Rates of Wages and Hours of Labour* or in *The Ministry of Labour Gazette*. We felt at an early stage of the work that the information on juveniles available to us from these two sources would not be sufficient to enable us to calculate separate indices for juveniles by industry, and we decided to exclude juveniles altogether from our indices. The indices, therefore, relate to adult rates only.[1]

The rates available for each industry or group of industries reflect the form of wage fixing by the Statutory authorities or the collective bargain made between employers and Trade Unions. In some industries one or two national rates only are specified; in others there is great detail providing for a wide range of grades of labour, for variations in different areas of the country, and for special circumstances in which the work is done. Sometimes this difference in the range of rates available reflects a real difference in the degree of differentiation of rates paid in the industries concerned, but in others it merely reflects an institutional difference about what is provided for in the national agreement and what is left for negotiation at the district, firm or workshop level. Unless these local variations reflect local agreements by independent District Trade Unions they are not usually included in the Ministry of Labour publications. In general, the most important point is that the rates provided for in separate workshops or firm agreements are rarely included.

The number of series varies substantially from industry to industry, and there is no relation between the importance of an industry and the number of series included. The total of separate rates taken into account in the indices is about 4,000. There is only one series for Agriculture in England and Wales outside Holland with Boston in Lincolnshire, but 136 series for Bricks and 188 for Printing.[2] A summary of the number of series used in the index is given in Table III.

Rates fixed by Statutory authorities apply of course to

---

[1] The age at which juveniles graduate to adult rates varies substantially over time and between occupations and industries. It will be seen, however, from Table VII, that the exclusion of juveniles makes little difference to the overall index.

[2] A detailed description of the rates included for each industry has been compiled, but it would take far too much space to publish with this article. The list can, however, be seen by anyone interested.

all those engaged in the relevant industries and occupations, but rates agreed by collective bargains in the first place relate only to members of the employers associations with whom the agreement is made.[1] The Unions may be in a position to induce other employers to follow the agreed rates, or they may even make specially favourable agreements with some of them; but there are some firms where rates are fixed without intervention or negotiation with the Unions. Without detailed and extensive research it is impossible to say, therefore, in the case of any particular set of rates, to what body of workers they apply in practice. Our indices are implicitly calculated on the basis that the collectively agreed rates apply to all wage-earners in the relevant industry.

There is, of course, the further point that both the Statutory rates and those collectively agreed, are minimum rates, and rates in excess of these may be paid even by firms who are members of the Employers' Association. It is quite common for those who are familiar with industrial conditions to quote cases they know where rates are paid in excess of what are called Trade Union or Statutory rates. But there is no regular information of the extent of the practice or of its variation from time to time. Since no account is taken of rates actually paid as distinct from rates laid down by agreement or order, our index must be interpreted, therefore, as an index of *minimum* rates collectively agreed or fixed by Statutory authorities.

For some industries there are both rates fixed by Statutory authorities and rates fixed by collective bargaining. Where both sets of rates were complete and easily manageable we have included both. Where the collective bargain included complicated local agreements[2] we have used the Statutory rates only. And where Statutory wage-fixing seems to have died out[3] during our period, we have used only the negotiated rates throughout.

---

[1] A rate awarded on the reference of a dispute to the Industrial Disputes (formerly National Arbitration) Tribunal may, however, be held to apply to the whole class of workers, whether or not Trade Union members or employed in Non-Federated firms. Similarly, a rate determined by normal collective agreement may, on application, be ordered by the Tribunal to apply to a firm not formally party to the agreement.

[2] As in Baking.

[3] As in Tobacco Manufacture.

The inclusion of rates for piece rate workers, or workers on any other kind of incentive bonus scheme, raises particularly acute difficulties.

These schemes usually vary from firm to firm, and their complex structure in each case, together with technical, economic and managerial progress will have a great influence on changes in the pay which workers actually receive.[1] Statutory wage orders and Trade Union national agreements rarely take account of these complex factors, and usually merely specify the minimum wage which a piece-worker of average ability should earn. In wages fixed by Statutory orders the actual wage to be earned in a given period of time is usually specified. Quite often in negotiated rates, it is prescribed that piece-workers should earn a certain percentage above their own, or time-worker's basic rates. In some cases when time-rates are changed by a specific sum, the same amount is added to the prescribed minimum earnings for piece-rate workers. In those cases where the prescribed piece-worker's rate is simply a percentage addition to the time-rate our estimate for changes in piece-rates and time-rates will be the same, if this percentage remains unchanged. Where piece-rate workers are covered in these ways, in effect we are measuring changes in the prescribed time-rates for piece-rate workers, rather than changes in actual piece-work prices. Specification of changes in piece-work prices themselves, as distinct from prescribed earnings of piece-workers, is very rare either in Statutory wage orders or collective agreements. But occasionally agreements which specify increases in time-rates also state the percentage by which piece-work prices shall be increased.[2]

In some industries even though piece-work is of substantial importance, rates for piece-workers are not mentioned in the collective agreement; in such cases increases in piece-rates are negotiated at district or firm level. Coal mining is an example. In the period covered by our index piece-rate workers are mentioned only once[3] in national agreements. For all other

---

[1] This is specially important in the engineering group of industries.

[2] This happens, for example, in the cases of Dock Labour throughout the period covered by our index, and for the last two changes for workers in Heavy Chemicals.

[3] In November 1951.

changes, only time-rate workers are mentioned. Yet one knows from other information, particularly about average earnings in coal mining, that the changing rates for work agreed at the local pit level in effect imply substantial increases in piece-workers' rates over the period. The way in which we have dealt with this case is explained in detail later.[1] Here we are concerned to explain how tenuous is the available material on piece-rate changes. This is probably the most serious gap in the index. Indeed the index should probably be interpreted as an index of time-rate wages, rates for piece-workers being taken in the main as the prescribed time-rate for piece-rate workers.[2]

Another complication arises from payments in kind. We may measure changes either in minimum cash payments or in the full value of the minimum remuneration, including any paid in kind. The choice presents itself chiefly in Agriculture, Coal Mining and the Catering Trades. In these industries allowances in kind are of substantial importance and we have decided to include them. But there may be allowances in other industries which are not specified in agreements and those would not be covered.[3]

Our index measures changes in *weekly* wage rates. In practice the time unit in which rates are specified varies. There are one or two annual and monthly rates, and a large number of shift and hourly rates. All these, therefore, have to be translated into equivalent weekly terms. This inevitably introduces yet another arbitrary element into our figures of changes in rates. It also means that where the rate per shift or per hour is increased merely to offset a reduction in the number of shifts or hours per standard working week, this does not show as an increase in rates in our index. Similarly a reduction in the number of standard hours per week for workers on a weekly rate, is not counted as an increase in

[1] See pages 178–9.

[2] However, even if comprehensive material was available of changes in actual detailed complex piece-work prices and incentive bonus payments, there would still be the extremely difficult, and possibly unmanageable, problem of translating these into percentage change in *wage-rates*, as distinct from changes in the *actual earnings* of piece-rate workers.

[3] e.g. the extension of canteen meals, often subsidised by the firm, and of luncheon vouchers, are examples of important additions to money wage-rates over this period which are not covered by our index.

rates.[1] In fact, however, the length of the normal working week has changed little since 1948, which is when our index starts. The Ministry of Labour's index of normal weekly hours fell from 104·3 in December 1945 (June 1947 = 100) to 98·6 at the end of 1947 and was 98·0 at the beginning of 1956.[2]

The calculation of indices of changes in wage rates by industries necessarily involves an industrial classification and grouping of rates and changes in rates. In principle we have adopted the system used in the official Standard Industrial Classification. But the institutional structure of Trade Unions and Statutory wage-fixing authorities is not industrial, but a complex occupational and industrial mixture. One cannot fit this structure into the Standard Industrial Classification without doing considerable violence to the real facts of the wage system. The element of arbitrariness in the classification increases the more detailed the industrial groups used. Although we have calculated indices for all the Minimum List Headings in the Standard Industrial Classification, we publish here in the main only figures for the much wider Orders.[3] In relation to these Orders there is less room for criticism of the classification we have adopted.[4]

III

So far we have discussed the basic material we have used. We now turn to the problems that arise in working out from this material percentage changes in rates compared with 1948. As explained earlier, about 4.000 separate series are used in compiling the indices, and it would be quite impossible and

---

[1] In practice, of course, such a reduction in hours may mean a more than proportionate increase in the earning power of the workers. For if, as often happens, the number of hours actually worked remains unchanged, a bigger proportion will be paid at higher overtime rates. The Trade Unions may, therefore, bargain for higher effective rates either by asking for a higher weekly rate or by asking for the standard number of hours per week to be reduced.

[2] *Ministry of Labour Gazette*, September 1957, p. 330. A change in normal weekly hours since 1948 may, however, be important in particular industries.

[3] Figure are given for one or two industries in the larger Orders.

[4] An alternative classification would be according to Trade Union affiliations and grouping of wage-fixing authorities. But this would be of little use for economic analysis, since other statistics with which one wants to compare changes in wage rates, such as earnings, employment, production, are based on an industrial classification, and since 1948 on the Standard Industrial Classification.

inappropriate in an article of this kind to try to explain how each of these is derived from the original material. All that we attempt here is to indicate some of the main recurrent problems and to show how we have dealt with these, giving a few actual examples of our methods by way of illustration.

Since all comparisons are made with the average for 1948, the first task is to establish for each series the average rate to be used for 1948. Where there was no change in rates in 1948, there is usually no problem in establishing this base rate. Where some change occurred during the year, the average for the year 1948 is arrived at by adding up the rates in force for the whole or major part of each month of 1948, and dividing the sum by twelve. Where there is no ambiguity about the date of the change, this is usually no more than a matter of simple arithmetic. But in some cases, although the information available implies that a change took place some time during 1948, there is no indication in the published material of the actual date of change. Since the date of change affects the average for 1948, by which we have divided all subsequent rates to arrive at the series of yearly and monthly relatives it is important to get this right, and in all doubtful cases we have obtained information about the actual date of change from the negotiating body concerned.[1]

Sometimes both official and unofficial dates are given for the coming into effect of a change. For example an increase in the rates for workers in Jute manufacture was prescribed by a Wages Council order having legal effect on April 14th, 1948. A footnote, however, states that 'pending the issue of the Order giving them Statutory effect, these new rates have been by agreement, in operation since January 7th'.[2] In this and other similar cases we take the new rates to be in operation from January, even though they were not legally enforceable minima until April.

If a complete series were available for later periods for each occupation and industry of all the rates in existence in 1948, the calculation of percentage changes for each of these

[1] This problem of the timing of the change, also often arises in the later periods of the index. But since in these cases the effect on the index is only for the period within which the change might have fallen, we have not gone to great trouble to discover the exact timing of the change, except where the weight or the amount of change was substantial.

[2] *Ministry of Labour Gazette*, June 1948, p. 213.

would in principle be comparatively easy. A recurrent difficulty is that in the course of the period new rates appear and, less frequently, rates hitherto quoted cease to appear.

Take Asbestos Cement Manufacture as an example of a new set of rates, appearing for the first time in 1951. Before September 30, 1951, one occupation only—unskilled workers on day work—is quoted, with different rates for each of three groups of towns (2s 6d per hour in Group 1 towns, 2s 5d in Group 2, and 2s 4d in Group 3). On September 30, 1951, an increase of 3d an hour was reported. In 'Time Rates of Wages and Hours of Labour, October 1, 1951' four grades of occupations (Grades 0 to 3) appear for each group of towns. The lowest Grade 0 has rates of 2s 9d an hour (Group 1 towns), 2s 8d (Group 2 towns) and 2s 7d (Group 3 towns). It seems, therefore, that this occupational Grade 0 corresponds to the old 'unskilled labourers on day work', and on this assumption the new rates for that grade give increases compared with 1948 of 25·1 per cent in Group 1 towns, 26·1 per cent in Group 2 towns and 27·2 per cent in Group 3 towns. For the three higher occupational grades (Grades 1, 2 and 3) the rates were 1d, 2d and 3d an hour respectively higher than those for Grade 0 in each group of towns.[1] To include these new rates we have in some way to relate them to the base year 1948. This means deciding whether they represented rates previously in existence and separate from those for 'unskilled labourers', but now being published by the Ministry of Labour for the first time, or whether they really indicated the introduction of a new set of grades and the promotion of some workers, to whom the unskilled rate previously applied. We make the former assumption, partly because in earlier issues of 'Time Rates of Wages and Hours of Labour' footnotes to the rates for this industry indicated that 'there is a grading system under which differentials . . . are paid . . . to workers in certain occupations'. We, therefore, assimilate the new occupational grade to Grade 0, that is, we assume that the percentage change in rates between 1948 and September 1951 was the same as that we had worked out for Grade 0 or 'unskilled labourers'.

An example where we interpreted the evidence in the

[1] e.g. for Group 1 towns, the rates were 2s 10d, 2s 11d, and 3s per hour respectively for Grades 1, 2 and 3.

alternative way, i.e. as promotion of some workers to a new set of more highly paid grades, occurred with women's rates in Railway Workshops. Up to October 1, 1949, rates were quoted just for 'women on women's work', at 71s per week in London and 69s in 'other districts'. 'Time Rates of Wages and Hours of Labour, October 1, 1950' quotes rates for six groups of occupations, with separate rates for London and 'other districts'. All these rates are given as before under the general heading: 'Women, 21 years and over, on women's work'. The lowest of the six groups had rates, 71s (London) and 69s (other districts)—identical with the single rates quoted previously. The other groups had rates rising to 80s (London) and 78s (other districts) for the highest. We assume that all workers paid at these new rates had been paid at the old general rate, and, therefore, that this new system represented a real increase in rates for such workers.[1]

Similar problems, so to speak in reverse, occur when rates cease to be quoted. There are fewer cases of these than of new rates, but they raise the same kind of issue of how to splice the old and new information.

Another frequent source of dilemma is the luxuriant growth of additions to the basic weekly rate to meet special circumstances. Some of these additions compensate for unfavourable working conditions, such as night-shifts and overtime, or wet, dirty or dangerous work,[2] or for jobs involving exceptional travelling;[3] some recognize special industrial worth, such as good timekeeping;[4] and others give special additions for working on expensive materials[5] or for looking after an added number of machines,[6] or taking on extra responsibility.[7] These special additions are difficult to deal with, because they do not usually change proportionately with the basic rates and because some of them are abolished during the period

[1] The increase varying from 2s in Group 5 to 9s in Group 1.

[2] e.g., this is provided for in builders' rates.

[3] e.g., constructional engineers in London working on jobs involving exceptional travelling get a special addition.

[4] e.g., woolworkers in Leicester receive a good time-keeping bonus.

[5] e.g., worsted spinners in Yorkshire receive extra if they work in coloured wool.

[6] e.g., wool spinners in Scotland are paid extra for every mule tended in excess of two.

[7] e.g., warehouse workers in pottery get an extra sum if they 'have control of books and orders.'

in which we are interested. And it is rare for much information to be given about the number of workers who enjoy the benefit of such additions. But they are frequently an important element in wage-rates and we felt it would be a mistake to ignore them altogether. We have, therefore, tried to include them where there was circumstantial evidence that they have sustained and widespread application. But this frequently involves us in making quite heroic assumptions. Changes in rates due to cost of living sliding-scale arrangements are in general covered.

The only important set of additions which we have ignored completely are those for shift-work, night-work[1] and over-time. This is partly because there is a case in principle for confining the index to the measurement of changes in rates for the 'normal working week'. The inclusion of overtime rates would make an appreciable difference to the indices, especially if allowance were made for the varying number of hours worked at such overtime rates. But it is doubtful whether the inclusion of shift allowances would make much difference.

In some industries the rate varies with the length of time the worker has been in the occupation. Where there is a special rate for a short probationary period, say for three months, we have ignored it; but where the initial period is long, and is either sharply extended or curtailed after 1948, we have tried to take account of this. The rates for locomotive firemen in Railway Service is a good example. From September 1, 1947, to February 1948, the rates were 101s a week during the first and second years, 104s in the third and fourth, 110s for the fifth to the tenth, and 115s from the eleventh year onwards. By April 1, 1956, rates had increased to 155s in the first year, 165s in the second and 175s 6d from the third year onwards. Thus, between September 1947 and April 1956, rates for firemen had increased by 53 per cent and 63 per cent for the first and second year of service, by 69 per cent for the third and fourth years, by 60 per cent for the fifth to tenth years and by 53 per cent for the eleventh year onwards.

---

[1] In a few occupations separate minimum rates are quoted for shift and night workers. But usually night and shift allowances are given in footnotes, and it is not clear, unless one knows the industry well, to what occupations or sections they apply.

M

The importance of the first four or first ten years of service depends on how long the fireman usually spends in the occupation. Assuming he spends twenty-five years on average in this occupation, the increase in the rate for the eleventh year onwards is relevant for rather more than half his service; that for the fifth to the tenth for about a quarter, and none of the others for more than a tenth each. We decided, therefore, to ignore the first four years, and to use an average rate derived by combining the rates for the fifth to tenth years and the eleventh year onwards in the ratio of 1 to 2. This gives us a rate of 113s 4d for January 1948[1] compared with the rate of 175s 6d[2] on April 1, 1956, an increase of 55 per cent over this period.

There is frequent difficulty in dealing with piece-workers' rates. Where the rates specified are 'piece-work basis time-rates' per hour or per week, or the percentage by which the earnings of piece-workers of 'average ability' shall exceed the time rate, the calculation is done in the same way as the time-workers. In such cases the series are merely prescribed time rates for piece-workers, rather than measures of changes in actual piece-work rates. Where actual additions to piece-work prices are quoted, the calculation of a series is always difficult and some very odd results can emerge. Take coal-mining as an example. This situation in coalmining is probably unique, but can be taken as a warning of the extreme difficulty of dealing with piece-work on a realistic basis in a wage-rate index. In the national agreements between the NUM and the Coal Board since 1948, an increase for piece-workers has been specified only once.[3] Apart from this, piece-workers were not mentioned in national agreements. If one sticks literally to the measurement of nationally agreed rates, therefore, there would be only a negligible percentage increase over the period for piece-workers in coalmining, and consequently a much lower increase in coalmining as a whole than the

---

[1] 110s (the fifth to tenth years) plus 2×115s (the eleventh and later years) divided by three.

[2] The rate for all years after the second.

[3] In the wage agreement of December 1951, which operated from November 22, 1951, a flat rate addition was granted to piece-workers of 2s 3d per shift for those underground and 1s 11d per shift for those on the surface; thus making, with the existing flat rate addition of 2s 8d, the total flat rate additions 4s 11d for underground piece-workers and 4s 7d for surface workers.

national average increase in rates. But this would be non-sensical, for it is generally known that prices for stints agreed at the pit level have been going up gradually over the whole period. The National Coal Board has tried to assess the importance of these upward revisions by getting quarterly reports from their Divisions of the estimated effect of piece-rate revisions at each colliery on the annual wages bill. The Board has given us access to these reports and we have used them to calculate an estimate of changes in piece-workers' rates for our period. The index figure so derived was very low compared with 144·0 in the rate index for time-workers, and with the increase in average earnings of all adult coalminers of 64 per cent between 1948 and 1955. We did not feel, therefore, that index for piece-work coalminers derived from the National Coal Board data was a sufficiently meaningful measure of changes in rates for those workers to warrant its use in the index. Consequently we were left with no satisfactory measure of changes in piece-work rates in coalmining, and had to fall back on the expedient of using the rate for time-workers only as a measure for the industry as a whole.[1] This example makes it worth emphasizing once again how unsatisfactory the treat ment of piece-rates is, both in the basic material and in our indices.

IV

After figures of percentage changes in rates for individual occupations have been calculated from the basic material, they have to be combined to give indices for industries, Orders and the economy as a whole. In principle we have followed the usual method of weighting by the wages bill. It was the availability of information for weighting which led us to make 1948 the starting point and base year for our index. For substantial information about wages bills is given in the first full post-war Census of Production for 1948, and the Ministry of Labour used the Standard Industrial Classification in their half-yearly Earnings Enquiries from October 1948, onwards. The index published here is base weighted, but we intend

[1] An alternative, in this and similar cases of difficulty, would have been to use estimates of figures of average actual earnings of piece-workers if they were available. But this would have meant departing from the basic concepts behind an index of *wage-rates*, and would in any case be inappropriate for one of the major uses we have in mind—the comparison of movements of rates with movements of actual earnings.

later to calculate a current year weighted index from the same material, in order to assess the effect on average rates of movements between industries.

Weighting raised another set of problems. But before turning to deal with these, it is worth mentioning that errors in weighting are usually less serious in their consequences in an index number of wage-rates than in other index numbers, such as those for prices or production. This is because weighting is more important if the movement in individual series included in the index differs substantially. If they all show a similar percentage change, any average, whatever set of weights is used, will give much the same index. In general, wage rates in different occupations tend to move much more together than the production or prices of individual commodities; and the problem of weighting, is therefore, less serious, especially for group indices which cover a large number of series. But since we are interested in constructing an index not merely to give an average for the whole economy but also to reveal any differences that there are between major industries, we have tried to be as accurate as possible in the weighting used.

We deal first with the problems of combining the individual series to give indices for each industry, and then with those of combining the industries into Orders and into an index for the economy as a whole.

Within an industry weighting is needed chiefly between piece-workers and time-workers, between different areas and sections of the industry, and between different occupations. Accurate figures of wages bills are not available for any of these categories and some substitute form of weighting has to be used.

Information by industry of the number of workers paid on some form of 'payment by results' scheme is given for October 1949.[1] Weighting on the basis of number of workers would underweight piece-workers, since generally the average earnings of piece-workers are higher than time-workers. We adjust the figures based on numbers to allow for this.[2]

---

[1] *Ministry of Labour Gazette*, March 1950, p. 86.

[2] The adjustment was made on the basis of the excess over the minimum time rates which piece-workers were normally entitled to earn under the wage agreement for the industry concerned.

For weighting areas and regions, the Census of Production, 1948, is very useful; for each Report analyses the wages bill of the Trade by Standard Regions. But these regions do not usually correspond to the regional differentiation of wage-rates. The distinction between 'London' rates and those for 'other districts' is a common one, but in the Census Classification London is included in the 'London and South Eastern Region'. We use the wages bill for that region to correspond to London, with the consequences that we persistently, if slightly, overweight movements in London rates in the indices.

In some industries all localities are assigned to grades, each with different rates. The weighting of such grades is a complicated task, especially if localities are continually being moved from one grade to another. Rates in building are a good example. In 1948 all towns outside Greater London and Merseyside were divided into four grades, A, A1, A2 and A3. Nearly every region had towns in each grade, so that regional wages bills do not help in weighting the grades. In addition every year some towns were moved from lower to higher grades, while the rates for each grade also rose steadily. In these circumstances the average of the movements of the rates for each grade would not adequately represent the course of wage-rates over the period. In October 1949, for instance, several towns were moved upward from Grade A3 to Grade A2. At that date the rates for craftsmen were 2s 8½d an hour in Grade A3 and 2s 9d an hour in Grade A2. For craftsmen in the regraded town this was effectively an increase in the rate of ½d an hour. To deal with this we construct separate series for towns moved from one grade to another, as well as for those which remained throughout in the same grade, and weight each series by the population of the towns to which they apply[1] in order to obtain a general rate for craftsmen.

Weighting of occupations is difficult unless, as sometimes happens, the industry itself publishes statistics of employment by occupations.[2] The Census of Population occupational analysis is relevent only for a few industries. For some of the

---

[1] On the assumption that the number of building workers varies with population size.

[2] As British Railways, in the Annual Reports of the British Transport Commission.

important industries special information was obtained, including rough estimates made for us by those with specialized knowledge of the industry.[1] But in many cases, no information even of the roughest kind is available, and in these cases we merely take an unweighted arithmetic average of the series for the various occupations.

In general we are able to weight individual industries by wages bills, to give series for Orders, although, as will be seen for some industries, these are only rough estimates. Estimating wages bills for industries covered by the Census of Production for 1948 is relatively straightforward. We allow for small firms and unsatisfactory returns by using the information about employment,[2] and for Northern Ireland on the basis of the Census of Production for 1949.

When two or three of our wage-rate industries are covered by a single Census of Production Trade, they are weighted by the wages bills of the appropriate specialist producers, or by the output of appropriate principal products given in the Census reports. Sometimes, although only one industry corresponds to a Census Trade, it seems unreasonable to give that industry the whole weight of the Trade. For example, the Census Trade 'Non-Ferrous Metals Smelting and Rolling' covers aluminium, magnesium, lead, zinc, tin and all other non-precious metals, other than iron and steel; but our wage-rate index for the industry covers 'Brass and Copper Rolling and Casting' only. We have no reason to believe that wage-rates for employees working with the other non-ferrous metals move closely with those on brass and copper, and, therefore, we have given our rate for the industry a weight corresponding to the wages bill of specialist producers of copper and brass. This is an example of a recurrent problem. Where only a section of an occupation, industry, or Order is covered by the wage-rate information, should one give the series the full weight of the occupation, industry or Order, or a weight corresponding only to that part actually covered? The first alternative implies the assumption that the rates not covered in the occupation, industry or Order move in close

---

[1] We have had access to statistics giving an occupational analysis of employees in Coal-mining and Cotton Spinning, and rough estimates in Building, Chemicals and Shipbuilding.

[2] We assume that the ratio of wages-bills of 'small' to 'large' firms is the same as that for employment.

correspondence with the average of the rates covered in that occupation, industry or Order; the second that the parts not covered are best represented by the average movement in a wider section of industry. In the particular example outlined above, we are virtually assuming that rates in non-ferrous metals manufacture, other than copper and brass, are better covered by the average index for the Order 'Metal Manufacture' than by the index for 'Copper and Brass', which forms part of the Order.

With the help of information supplied by the Central Statistical Office, we have been able to arrive at fairly reliable estimates for relative size of wages bills for the various industries in Agriculture,[1] Public Administration[2] and Transport.[3] For Distribution we use the information about wages and salary bills for various kinds of business, wholesale and retail, published in the Reports of the Census of Distribution and Other Services 1950. The weighting of the industries we cover under Miscellaneous Services[4] is done more crudely, mainly on the basis of information about employment.[5]

In combining the indices for Orders to give an index for the economy as a whole, we use the figures of wages bills for 1948 given in the Blue Book, National Income and Expenditure.[6]

For every Order, except 'Miscellaneous Services', the wages bill for the whole Order is used as a weight in arriving at the total index, even though in many cases some industries within the Order are not adequately covered. As was explained earlier, this amounts to an assumption that the rates in the industries concerned are more likely to have moved as the average of the rest of the Order than as the average for the economy as a whole. Such an assumption does not seem to be warranted in the case of the 'Miscellaneous Services'

[1] Agriculture and Forestry.

[2] National Government Service and Local Government Service.

[3] Post Office, Railway Service, Road Transport, Road Haulage, Merchant Navy, Dock Labour, Inland Waterways and Cold Storage.

[4] Catering, Hairdressing, Laundering, Funeral Direction, Cinemas, Theatres and Musicians in theatres and music halls.

[5] Since men earn more than women, we take account of differences in the proportion of male and female employees.

[6] For 'Distribution' and 'Other Services' figures are given in the Blue Book only for 'income from employment' (wages and salaries combined), but with help from the Central Statistical Office estimates were made of the wages-bill.

Order; firstly because the industries for which we have rates cover only about half the wages bill of the Order, and secondly because there seems to be no significant economic relation between them and those not covered.[1] In this case we have given the Order a weight in the total index represented only by the wages bill for those industries for which wage rates are included.

Throughout the index, for the industries, Orders and the total index, we calculate separate series for men and women. To combine these to give the indices for all workers, we need weights, and here again in principle we use the wages bill of men and women employees. In practice such figures are not always available, and sometimes we have to use estimates of numbers of men and women employed, corrected roughly for the difference between the average earnings of men and women.

Information about rates for women is not always available. In such cases, in calculating the Order index, we use the index for men only as the index for 'all workers' for the industry, thus assuming that women's rates in those industries which are not covered in our figures are best taken in each case to move together with those for men. But in arriving at the index for women for any particular Order we merely take account of the available women's indices for industries included within the Order, thus assuming that women's rates in the Order not covered are best represented by the average of those which are covered.

v

The main results are given in Tables IV (All Workers), V (Men), and VI (Women). These give annual figures for 1948 to 1955 and certain monthly figures from the beginning of 1955 until April 1956, for all the Orders of the Standard Industrial Classification, together with figures for a few of the more important industries within the largest Orders. The weights used are shown in each table.

[1] The industries covered are Cinemas, Theatres and Music Halls, Catering, Laundries, Hairdressing and Funeral Direction; those not covered, Sport, other Recreation and Betting, Private Domestic Service, Photography, Welfare and Charitable Services, Community Services, Services in Colonial, Dominion and Foreign Governments, Chimney-Sweeping and Window-Cleaning.

The movement in our indices, for the total, men and women, both for all industries and manufacturing industries separately, correspond very closely with the Ministry of Labour indices for the period (see Table VII).

The average increase over the period is 54 per cent for men and 53 per cent for women. However, in every Order, except Treatment of Non-Metalliferous Mining Products and Professional Services, women's rates have increased by as much as, or by more than, men's.[1] The equality of the overall increase for the two indices reflects the much heavier weight in the women's than in the men's index of the industries where rates have risen least. The indices for women range from 138 for Cotton to 177 for Vehicles. In general, rates have risen well above the average in the Vehicles, Engineering and Metal Goods industries, but these three Orders together account for only 8.3 per cent of the weights in the index for women. The important Orders for women are Textiles, Clothing, Distribution and Miscellaneous Services (accounting together for 63·4 per cent of the weights),[2] and in these rates rose by only 47 per cent, 52 per cent, 55 per cent and 43 per cent respectively.

The spread of increases for men—from 139 in Cotton to 164 in Gas, Water and Electricity—was narrower than for women. Here again the high increases in Metal Manufacture and Engineering are outstanding. One or two industries, such as Textiles, which tend to lag behind later, are well up to the average rate of increase in 1954.

One of the most interesting and remarkable features of post-war movements in wages is the wide divergence between the rates of increase of wage-rates and average wage-earnings. Complete figures of average earnings are not available for all industries, but such figures as there are are given in Tables VIII (All Workers), IX (Men), and X (Women) in the form of index numbers (with 1948 = 100) to facilitate comparisons with changes in rates. These index numbers are based on the actual earnings and employment in industries at each date, so they reflect the changing composition of the labour force

[1] These comparisons and those made later in this section may be affected by the year, 1948, taken as the base. In a later article a more detailed comparison which will allow for this possibility, will be made.

[2] See Table III for the relative importance, by wages-bills, of women's rates in each Order.

within each industry or group of industries. The figures are mainly based on the half-yearly Earnings Enquiries taken by the Ministry of Labour, but, although they are on a slightly different basis, figures from other sources have been used for Agriculture and Coal Mining. Important sections of the economy are not covered by these figures,[1] and we felt, therefore, that it would be misleading to work out an overall average earnings index[2] to compare with our overall index of wage-rates.

In making comparisons between rates and earnings for particular industries, it is important to keep in mind the simple point, frequently overlooked, that the indices of wage rates and of earnings merely *compare rates of change* in different industries, and tell us nothing about the absolute level of rates or earnings in one industry compared with another. Similarly a comparison of indices of wage-rates and average earnings for an industry gives no indication of the absolute margin between minimum rates and actual earnings in that industry. It merely measures the difference in the relative movement of minimum rates and earnings.

The interesting aspect of the divergence between movements of rates and earnings which our calculations make it possible to analyse for the first time, is the variation between industries. The variation is substantial. For men it is narrowest in Gas, Electricity and Water (rates in April 1956, 164, average earnings 170) and widest in Building (rates 153, average earnings 181). The variation for women is peculiar. In some industries the increase in average earnings over the period is actually less than the increase in rates,[3] and in the remainder the divergence is much narrower than for men. Although in nearly every industry the index of rates for women shows an increase as great as or greater than that for men, average earnings of women in all industries except one have risen substantially less than for men. We leave any attempt to explain this and other interesting aspects of the relation between rates and earnings to a later article.

[1] Distribution, Catering, Entertainment, Commerce, Domestic Service and a large part of Transport are not included.

[2] We hope in the later article to make an estimate of movements of overall average earnings covering all wage-earners.

[3] This is true in Building, Metals, Engineering, Vehicles, Agriculture, Leather Goods, and Manufacturers of Wood.

TABLE I

IMPORTANCE OF STATUTORY AND NON-STATUTORY WAGE RATES

Percentage of 'Weight' in each Order covered by Statutory and Non-Statutory Rates

SIC ORDER	TOTAL		MEN		Per cent WOMEN	
	Statutory Rates	Non-Statutory Rates	Statutory Rates	Non-Statutory Rates	Statutory Rates	Non-Statutory Rates
TOTAL	22	78	18	82	46	54
I. Agricultural, Forestry and Fishing	92	8	92	8	94	6
II. Mining and Quarrying	—	100	—	100	—	100
III. Treatment of Non-Metalliferous Mining Products	—	100	—	100	—	100
IV. Chemicals and Allied Trades ...	—	100	—	100	—	100
V. Metal Manufacture	—	100	—	100	—	100
VI. Engineering, Shipbuilding and Electrical Goods	—	100	—	100	—	100
VII. Vehicles	1	99	1	99	10	90
VIII. Metal Goods N.E.S.	53	47	47	53	70	30
IX. Precision Instruments, Jewellery, etc.	—	100	—	100	—	100
X. Textiles	12	88	7	93	16	84
XI. Leather, Leather Goods and Fur	18	82	15	85	42	58
XII. Clothing	66	34	58	42	72	28
XIII. Food, Drink and Tobacco ...	49	51	47	53	55	45
XIV. Manufactures of Wood and Cork	5	95	5	95	6	94
XV. Paper and Printing	10	90	7	93	30	70
XVI. Other Manufacturing Industries	19	81	14	86	34	66
XVII. Building and Contracting ...	—	100	—	100	—	100
XVIII. Gas, Water and Electricity ...	—	100	—	100	—	100
XIX. Transport and Communication...	14	86	14	86	—	100
XX. Distributive Trades	37	63	31	69	50	50
XXII. Public Administration and Defence	29	71	29	71	50	50
XXIII. Professional Services	—	100	—	100	—	100
XXIV. Miscellaneous Services	73	27	74	26	75	25

TABLE II

INDUSTRIES FOR WHICH NO RATES ARE INCLUDED IN THE INDEX

SIC ORDER	SIC Minimum List Headings Not Covered	Percentage of Order by 'Weight'
I. Agriculture, Forestry and Fishing ...	3 Fishing	...
IV. Chemicals and Allied Trades	36 Mineral Oil Refining	3
VII. Vehicles	82 Aircraft Manufacture and Repair 85 Other Locomotive Manufacture	} 16
VIII. Metal Goods N.E.S.	91 Bolts, Nuts and Screws	11
XVI. Other Manufacturing Industries ...	194 Miscellaneous Stationers' Goods 199 Miscellaneous Manufacturing Industries	} 21
XIX. Transport and Communication	222 Other Road Passenger Transport 227 Air Transport ... ... 238 Other Transport and Communication	} 6
XXI. Insurance, Banking and Finance ...	250 Insurance, Banking and Finance ...	100
XXIII. Professional Services	270 Accountancy ... ... 271 Education ... ... 272 Law ... ... 274 Religion ... ... 275 Other Professional and Business Services	} ...[1]
XXIV. Miscellaneous Services ...	281 Sport, Other Recreations and Betting ... ... 287 Dry Cleaning, Job Dyeing, Carpet Beating, etc.... ... ... 291 Private Domestic Service (Resident) 299 Other Services[2]	} 45

[1] The only MLH covered is 'Medical and Dental Services'.
[2] Funeral Direction which is part of this MLH is covered.

TABLE III

NUMBER OF SERIES INCLUDED IN THE INDEX

SIC ORDER	Rates for Men	Rates for Women	Percentage weight given to Women's Rates in Order
TOTAL	**3,024**	**828**	**15·5[1]**
I. Agriculture, Forestry and Fishing... ...	25	11	8·7
II. Mining and Quarrying	93	—	—
III. Treatment of Non-Metalliferous Mining Products	275	36	11·6
IV. Chemicals and Allied Trades	132	42	13·7
V. Metal Manufacture	62	3	3·1
VI. Engineering, Shipbuilding and Electrical Goods	162	18	8·2
VII. Vehicles	176	30	3·8
VIII. Metal Goods N.E.S.	147	42	25·3
IX. Precision Instruments, Jewellery, etc. ...	43	18	20·5
X. Textiles	258	196	40·9
XI. Leather, Leather Goods and Fur	36	21	13·1
XII. Clothing	139	94	54·7
XIII. Food, Drink and Tobacco	205	58	22·4
XIV. Manufacture of Wood and Cork	144	35	9·2
XV. Paper and Printing	233	41	15·4
XVI. Other Manufacturing Industries	50	33	22·7
XVII. Building and Contracting	118	4	0·2
XVIII. Gas, Water and Electricity	243	—	1·2
XIX. Transport and Communication	151	4	4·8
XX. Distributive Trades	194	69	31·9
XXII. Public Administration and Defence ...	30	2	0·9
XXIII. Professional Services	20	16	62·4
XXIV. Miscellaneous Services	88	55	58·1

[1] The figure of the proportion of women employed in the labour force is much higher, but average earnings of women overall are only about half those of men.

TABLE IV

WAGE RATE INDEX BY INDUSTRIES
ALL ADULT WORKERS[1]
AVERAGE 1948 = 100

SIC Order		I	II	III	IV	V	VI			VII	VIII	IX	X	
	Total All Industries	Agriculture, Forestry and Fishing	Mining and Quarrying	Treatment of Non-Metalliferous Mining Products	Chemical and Allied Trades	Metal Manufacture	Total Shipbuilding, Engineering and Electrical Goods	Shipbuilding	Engineering	Vehicles	Metal Goods N.E.S.	Precision Instruments, Jewellery, etc.	Total Textiles	Cotton
Weights	1000	56	79	19	18	39	102	14	74	61	25	7	46	14
Annual														
1949	102·8	103·6	100·2	102·9	102·6	103·8	103·8	103·8	104·0	102·8	103·2	101·4	104·7	104·4
1950	104·7	105·2	101·2	104·6	105·8	105·6	105·1	105·7	105·1	103·0	105·2	103·0	108·0	106·4
1951	113·4	112·5	111·7	113·7	115·4	115·6	114·4	114·6	114·8	111·4	113·1	109·7	118·4	118·8
1952	123·4	122·1	123·9	124·5	126·5	125·4	125·8	125·8	126·2	122·0	124·9	119·3	126·5	123·0
1953	129·1	127·8	128·0	130·1	131·4	129·6	131·7	131·8	132·0	128·4	131·5	124·4	131·5	125·9
1954	134·7	133·2	134·1	135·1	136·8	135·6	137·3	137·7	137·7	134·5	136·4	130·1	136·0	131·8
1955	143·3	140·7	143·9	144·5	146·1	147·0	146·3	147·9	145·9	143·1	146·0	137·8	142·6	138·1
Monthly														
1955—Jan.	137·8	133·9	134·2	137·6	140·2	138·7	138·8	139·7	138·8	138·9	141·1	135·3	139·9	137·4
April	141·8	141·2	145·9	142·8	146·0	141·3	147·4	149·6	146·9	138·9	144·5	135·7	140·7	138·1
Oct.	145·6	141·4	147·2	147·3	147·9	150·7	148·2	149·6	147·6	145·7	148·9	139·1	144·3	138·1
Dec.	146·4	141·8	147·2	147·7	148·0	151·5	148·2	149·6	147·7	145·7	150·3	142·6	145·6	138·6
1956—Jan.	147·3	141·8	147·3	147·7	148·1	152·4	148·3	149·6	147·7	145·7	151·6	146·1	146·0	138·6
Feb.	149·8	148·6	157·4	148·8	153·0	152·4	148·8	149·6	148·1	153·9	152·6	147·4	146·5	138·6
March	152·4	150·6	158·7	150·0	154·4	154·6	158·8	161·1	158·4	154·7	153·2	147·4	146·5	138·6
April	153·7	150·6	158·9	153·0	155·3	162·0	159·0	161·1	158·5	156·1	155·0	148·4	147·1	138·6

[1] Men and Women, i.e. excluding Juveniles

XI	XII	XIII	XIV	XV	XVI	XVII		XVIII	XIX	XX	XXII	XXIII	XXIV
Leather, Leather Goods and Fur	Clothing	Food, Drink and Tobacco	Manufactures of Wood and Cork	Paper and Printing	Other Manufacturing Industries	Total Building and Contracting	Building	Gas, Water and Electricity	Transport and Communications	Distributive Trades	Public Administration and Defence	Professional Services	Miscellaneous Services
4	27	37	17	24	11	114	78	20	98	80	29	12	75
105·1	103·7	103·9	104·0	102·9	103·3	102·5	102·3	103·3	100·9	102·2	103·5	103·2	103·3
106·6	104·5	105·8	106·4	106·7	104·4	105·2	104·9	106·4	101·7	105·6	104·8	103·2	106·2
113·7	111·4	113·9	116·3	117·2	114·4	114·0	113·4	114·7	111·4	114·6	111·4	111·9	111·1
122·9	117·9	124·5	129·2	132·6	122·5	124·3	123·8	124·4	119·6	124·1	122·4	120·4	118·1
130·2	125·0	130·4	135·4	138·0	127·1	131·0	130·5	130·8	124·4	130·5	126·5	124·5	124·8
134·5	132·2	135·4	140·1	140·2	133·1	137·3	136·9	136·2	131·4	135·9	134·3	129·2	128·7
140·7	138·9	144·2	148·6	146·9	140·9	145·8	145·3	148·7	140·7	144·3	142·3	138·5	135·3
137·3	136·2	140·9	143·5	144·4	134·5	139·7	139·2	143·4	137·0	140·5	137·3	132·9	130·0
137·3	137·8	141·7	146·1	145·0	138·9	141·7	140·7	150·4	138·4	143·6	139·1	132·9	134·5
144·8	142·3	146·7	153·4	149·4	142·5	148·3	147·9	150·4	146·7	145·7	145·7	142·5	136·9
145·2	142·7	147·6	153·6	149·6	149·2	148·6	147·9	150·4	144·6	148·8	145·7	142·5	137·2
145·2	145·6	148·8	155·1	155·8	149·5	148·6	147·9	156·2	144·6	148·8	151·9	142·5	138·8
145·2	145·8	148·8	155·8	155·8	149·5	151·6	151·1	163·5	145·0	149·3	152·6	142·5	138·9
145·2	146·2	150·5	157·1	155·8	150·8	152·2	151·1	163·7	148·3	151·8	157·0	152·9	142·4
145·2	148·6	153·8	159·1	156·3	151·4	152·6	151·1	163·7	150·2	153·6	160·6	152·9	142·5

TABLE V

WAGE RATE INDEX BY INDUSTRIES
MEN
AVERAGE 1948 = 100

SIC Order		I	II	III	IV	V	VI			VII	VIII	IX	X	
	Total All Industries	Agriculture, Forestry and Fishing	Mining and Quarrying	Treatment of Non-Metalliferous Mining Products	Chemical and Allied Trades	Metal Manufacture	Total Shipbuilding, Engineering and Electrical Goods	Shipbuilding	Engineering	Vehicles	Metal Goods N.E.S.	Precision Instruments, Jewellery, etc.	Total Textiles	Cotton
Weights	1000	61	94	20	19	45	111	16	79	69	24	6	31	8
Annual														
1949	102·7	103·6	100·2	102·9	102·4	103·7	103·7	103·8	103·9	102·8	103·2	101·4	104·7	104·4
1950	104·4	105·2	101·2	104·5	105·6	105·6	104·9	105·7	104·9	102·9	105·3	103·0	107·7	106·5
1951	113·2	112·4	111·7	113·5	115·0	115·5	114·1	114·6	114·3	111·4	113·0	109·7	117·7	118·8
1952	123·4	122·0	123·9	124·5	126·1	125·4	125·1	125·8	125·2	121·9	123·9	119·3	126·2	122·9
1953	128·9	127·7	128·0	130·2	131·0	129·5	130·8	131·8	130·9	127·8	130·4	124·4	131·4	126·3
1954	134·5	133·1	134·1	135·2	136·3	135·5	136·4	137·7	136·4	133·7	135·2	129·9	135·2	131·5
1955	143·4	140·7	143·9	144·9	145·4	146·8	146·2	147·8	145·9	142·4	144·6	137·5	142·0	138·2
Monthly														
1955—Jan.	137·8	133·8	134·2	137·7	139·6	138·6	138·6	139·7	138·7	138·2	139·5	134·9	139·1	137·4
April	142·2	141·2	145·9	143·0	145·4	141·1	147·2	149·6	146·7	140·0	143·4	135·4	140·3	138·2
Oct.	145·7	141·4	147·2	147·7	147·2	150·6	148·0	149·6	147·4	144·9	147·3	138·8	143·8	138·2
Dec.	146·5	141·8	147·2	148·2	147·3	151·4	148·1	149·6	147·5	144·9	148·7	142·1	145·2	138·7
1956—Jan.	147·3	141·8	147·3	148·2	147·5	152·4	148·1	149·6	149·6	144·9	149·8	145·4	145·7	138·7
Feb.	150·5	148·7	157·4	149·3	152·1	152·1	148·6	149·6	149·6	153·2	151·0	146·7	146·6	138·7
March	152·7	150·6	158·7	150·7	153·6	154·5	158·6	161·1	157·9	153·8	153·6	146·7	146·6	138·7
April	154·1	150·6	158·9	153·8	154·5	161·9	158·8	161·1	158·2	155·2	153·6	147·6	146·7	138·7

XI	XII	XIII	XIV	XV	XVI	XVII		XVIII	XIX	XX	XXII	XXIII	XXIV
Leather, Leather Goods and Fur	Clothing	Food, Drink and Tobacco	Manufactures of Wood and Cork	Paper and Printing	Other Manufacturing Industries	Total Building and Contracting	Building	Gas, Water and Electricity	Transport and Communications	Distributive Trades	Public Administration and Defence	Professional Services	Miscellaneous Services
4	15	35	18	23	11	135	92	23	111	65	34	5	41
104·5	102·8	103·4	104·0	102·9	103·3	102·5	102·3	103·3	100·9	102·2	103·5	103·6	104·1
105·9	103·8	105·2	106·4	106·5	104·3	105·2	104·9	106·4	101·6	105·3	104·8	103·6	107·0
113·0	109·8	113·3	116·2	116·8	114·2	114·0	113·4	114·7	111·4	113·4	111·4	112·5	111·5
121·6	116·9	123·7	128·9	131·7	121·9	124·3	123·8	124·4	119·6	123·4	122·4	121·2	118·1
128·6	123·1	129·5	135·2	137·1	126·2	131·0	130·5	130·8	124·3	129·2	126·5	125·4	125·0
132·6	129·3	134·3	139·8	139·2	132·3	137·3	136·9	136·2	130·8	134·7	134·3	130·2	128·4
138·8	135·7	143·1	148·1	145·8	140·0	145·8	145·3	148·7	140·5	143·6	142·3	139·5	135·1
135·3	132·7	139·9	143·2	143·5	133·5	139·7	139·2	143·4	137·5	140·0	137·2	133·9	130·1
135·3	135·0	140·6	145·8	143·9	138·4	141·7	140·7	150·4	138·8	143·0	139·0	133·9	135·5
143·0	138·4	145·4	152·4	148·2	141·2	148·3	147·9	150·4	141·6	146·2	145·7	143·5	136·1
143·2	138·7	146·0	152·5	148·3	148·6	148·6	147·9	150·4	144·3	148·2	145·7	143·5	136·6
143·2	141·2	147·4	154·0	154·1	148·9	148·6	147·9	156·2	144·3	148·2	151·8	143·5	138·8
143·2	141·2	147·4	154·6	154·1	148·9	151·6	151·1	163·5	148·0	148·7	152·5	143·5	139·1
143·2	141·7	149·0	155·9	154·1	150·0	152·2	151·1	163·7	148·1	151·2	156·9	143·5	141·4
143·2	145·1	152·8	157·7	154·5	150·4	152·6	151·1	163·7	149·8	153·0	159·9	154·1	141·5

N

TABLE VI

WAGE RATE INDEX BY INDUSTRIES
WOMEN
AVERAGE 1948 = 100

SIC Orders			III	IV	V	VI			VII	VIII	IX	X	
	Total All Industries	Agriculture, Forestry and Fishing	Treatment of Non-Metalliferous Mining Products	Chemical and Allied Trades	Metal Manufacture	Total Engineering, Shipbuilding and Electrical Goods	Shipbuilding	Engineering	Vehicles	Metal Goods N.E.S.	Precision Instruments, Jewellery, etc.	Total Textiles	Cotton
Weights	1000	31	14	14	9	55	1	49	19	29	8	123	48
Annual													
1949	103·4	103·8	102·4	103·6	104·7	104·4	103·9	104·6	103·6	103·2	100·2	104·7	104·3
1950	106·0	105·5	105·5	106·9	107·0	106·4	105·5	106·6	104·5	105·1	101·5	108·3	106·3
1951	114·4	113·3	114·5	117·5	119·4	118·8	114·6	119·4	112·4	113·5	108·7	119·1	118·9
1952	123·7	122·7	124·4	128·3	133·5	134·4	124·0	135·2	124·6	128·0	118·3	127·0	123·0
1953	130·5	128·4	129·7	133·5	141·9	142·1	124·0	143·1	141·4	135·5	123·8	132·1	126·5
1954	135·8	133·8	134·4	140·2	149·0	148·6	135·3	149·5	153·8	140·7	130·5	136·8	131·9
1955	143·6	140·9	141·9	150·0	163·2	159·8	147·6	160·7	161·9	150·1	139·3	143·3	138·0
Monthly													
1955—Jan.	139·0	134·3	136·3	144·1	151·4	151·1	139·0	152·0	157·1	145·8	137·8	140·9	137·5
April	141·8	141·4	141·3	149·9	163·2	161·3	149·3	162·1	157·8	147·6	137·8	141·7	138·0
Oct.	146·1	141·4	144·0	152·4	163·2	161·8	149·3	162·7	165·9	153·7	140·0	145·0	138·0
Dec.	147·1	141·8	144·0	152·6	161·3	161·9	149·3	162·7	165·9	155·3	145·2	146·1	138·5
1956—Jan.	148·2	141·8	144·0	153·0	163·2	161·9	149·3	162·7	165·9	157·1	151·2	146·4	138·5
Feb.	149·0	148·4	144·6	159·0	163·2	163·2	149·3	163·1	176·3	157·3	152·5	147·0	138·5
March	151·9	150·6	144·7	159·9	174·2	173·8	161·0	174·7	176·3	159·0	152·5	147·0	138·5
April	152·8	150·6	147·2	160·9	174·2	174·1	161·0	175·1	177·0	159·0	152·4	147·3	138·5

XI	XII	XIII	XIV	XV	XVI	XVII		XIX	XX	XXII	XXIII	XXIV
Leather, Leather Goods and Fur	Clothing	Food, Drink and Tobacco	Manufactures of Wood and Cork	Paper and Printing	Other Manufacturing Industries	Total Building and Contracting	Building	Transport and Communications	Distributive Trades	Public Administration and Defence	Professional Services	Miscellaneous Services
5	95	50	9	26	17	1	1	30	161	2	47	255
109·1	104·4	105·4	104·4	103·3	103·5	103·3	103·3	101·9	101·9	103·5	102·9	102·8
111·5	105·0	107·8	106·6	107·8	104·5	106·8	106·8	102·7	106·3	104·8	102·9	105·7
118·6	112·7	115·7	117·5	119·1	115·3	113·4	113·4	113·1	115·6	114·1	111·5	110·9
130·9	118·5	127·1	133·0	136·8	124·1	127·5	127·5	119·0	126·1	126·2	119·9	118·1
140·1	126·4	133·4	138·5	142·8	130·1	136·5	136·5	127·9	133·3	130·6	124·0	124·7
146·6	134·5	139·2	144·0	145·4	135·5	141·7	141·7	133·9	138·5	140·0	128·6	128·8
153·8	141·6	147·8	145·0	152·9	144·1	162·0	162·0	145·2	146·0	145·7	137·9	135·3
149·8	139·0	144·3	147·6	149·6	137·8	152·6	152·6	142·0	141·8	142·5	132·3	130·0
149·8	140·0	145·5	149·7	151·4	140·8	154·9	154·9	142·0	145·2	142·5	132·3	132·9
157·5	145·5	150·8	166·0	155·9	147·0	165·8	165·8	146·0	148·1	147·9	141·9	137·5
158·6	146·1	152·9	166·1	156·0	151·5	165·8	165·8	152·8	150·5	147·9	141·9	137·5
158·6	149·3	153·4	169·0	165·2	151·7	165·8	165·8	152·8	150·5	160·5	141·9	138·8
158·6	149·6	153·4	169·7	165·2	151·7	170·3	170·3	152·8	150·6	160·5	141·9	138·8
158·6	150·0	155·6	171·0	165·2	153·7	170·3	170·3	152·8	153·2	160·5	152·2	142·9
158·6	151·5	156·7	175·2	165·3	154·8	170·3	170·3	159·3	155·1	168·4	152·2	142·9

TABLE VII

MINISTRY OF LABOUR INDEX OF WAGE RATES COMPARED WITH THE 'MANCHESTER' INDEX
$1948 = 100$[1]

	ALL INDUSTRIES							MANUFACTURING INDUSTRIES		
	M. of L. Index		Manchester Index	M.of L. Index	Manchester Index	M.of L. Index	Manchester Index	M. of L. Index		Manchester Index
	All Workers including Juveniles	Adult Workers	Adult Workers	MEN		WOMEN		All Workers including Juveniles	Adult Workers	Adult Workers
Annual 1949	102·7	102·7	102·8	102·5	102·7	103·3	103·4	103·4	103·3	103·6
1950	104·7	104·6	104·7	104·3	104·4	106·0	106·0	105·2	105·1	105·3
1951	113·5	113·3	113·4	113·0	113·2	115·0	114·4	115·1	114·9	114·4
1952	122·8	122·5	123·4	122·2	123·4	124·1	123·7	124·9	124·5	124·9
1953	128·5	128·1	129·1	127·6	128·9	130·8	130·5	130·6	130·1	130·6
1954	134·1	133·6	134·7	133·2	134·5	136·2	135·8	136·1	135·5	136·0
1955	143·2	142·7	143·3	142·4	143·4	144·2	143·6	145·0	144·4	144·6
Monthly 1955 January	137·9	137·4	137·8	136·8	137·8	140·6	139·0	139·3	138·7	139·4
April	143·2	142·8	141·8	142·7	142·2	143·4	141·8	144·8	144·2	142·8
October	144·9	144·4	145·6	144·2	145·7	145·9	146·1	147·0	146·3	147·1
December	145·7	145·2	146·4	144·8	146·5	147·4	147·1	147·6	147·0	147·8
1956 January	147·6	147·0	147·3	146·7	147·3	149·0	148·2	149·0	148·3	148·7
February	149·1	148·6	149·8	148·3	150·5	150·2	149·0	149·5	148·8	150·4
March	153·1	152·5	152·4	152·3	152·7	153·6	151·9	155·3	154·5	153·4
April	155·0	154·3	153·7	154·2	154·1	154·8	152·8	156·5	155·7	155·3

[1] The original Ministry of Labour Index for the period to January 1956 is based on June 1947=100, and from February 1956 on January 1956=100. We have converted these to 1948=100, for comparison with our Index.

TABLE VIII

INDEX OF AVERAGE WEEKLY EARNINGS BY INDUSTRIES
ALL WORKERS[1]
AVERAGE 1948 = 100

SIC Order	I (³) Agriculture, Forestry and Fishing	II Mining and Quarrying	III Treatment of Non-Metalliferous Mining Products	IV Chemical and Allied Trades	V Metal Manufacture	VI Total Shipbuilding, Engineering and Electrical Goods	VI Shipbuilding	VI Engineering	VII Vehicles	VIII Metal Goods N.E.S.	IX Precision Instruments, Jewellery, etc.
Annual (²)											
1949	104·4	103·5	105·3	105·3	102·9	103·5	97·2	104·2	101·2	104·9	105·5
1950	107·0	108·2	109·8	111·0	107·9	107·9	99·7	109·1	106·5	110·8	110·2
1951	114·5	120·8	121·6	122·4	117·0	117·7	109·1	120·1	113·8	119·3	118·8
1952	123·1	133·2	130·9	130·1	127·5	129·8	122·0	131·5	123·6	130·4	128·8
1953	131·0	137·6	139·5	140·1	133·1	137·6	128·4	139·0	133·1	138·0	137·0
1954	139·1	145·8	148·4	149·1	143·7	147·2	136·1	150·3	143·0	147·6	144·7
1955	149·4	155·3	161·2	163·1	157·2	160·4	151·1	163·4	156·4	161·2	157·2
1955—April	147·0	154·7	158·8	161·4	154·9	159·2	150·3	162·0	155·1	159·1	156·2
October	151·8	165·5	163·5	164·7	159·4	161·5	151·9	164·9	157·7	163·3	162·5
1956—April	156·1	175·0	170·8	172·9	169·4	173·3	168·2	175·4	165·0	170·9	164·4

(¹) Including Juveniles.
(²) The 'Annual' figures are averages of the figures for April and October.
(³) The figures of earnings cover Agriculture only, and are a combination of the separate indexes for men and women weighted by wage-bills in 1948.
(⁴) Only that part of the order covered by the Ministry of Labour's Earnings Enquiries.

X		XI	XII	XIII	XIV	XV	XVI	XVII		XVIII	XIX	XXII
											(4)	(4)
Total Textiles	Cotton	Leather, Leather Goods and Fur	Clothing	Food, Drink and Tobacco	Manufacture of Wood and Cork	Paper and Printing	Other Manufacturing Industries	Total Building and Contracting	Building	Gas, Water and Electricity	Transport and Communications	Public Administration and Defence
106·5	105·9	102·8	107·3	105·2	104·9	105·9	102·3	105·0	105·2	103·3	104·4	107·5
113·2	110·6	106·6	111·3	108·6	111·0	110·9	108·1	111·3	111·1	107·5	106·9	109·6
125·5	126·1	114·2	118·2	118·0	123·1	122·0	119·4	125·4	124·6	118·8	118·2	119·7
128·0	120·9	118·4	123·3	127·1	130·9	134·1	125·8	134·5	133·9	127·9	126·2	129·5
140·1	134·3	127·3	133·0	133·6	139·4	144·2	135·6	143·8	143·4	134·2	132·6	136·0
148·3	144·0	133·1	138·1	141·6	147·4	152·1	145·0	152·2	151·3	142·4	143·0	142·2
156·5	148·2	142·8	147·5	153·8	158·3	164·5	157·4	166·9	166·1	158·8	159·8	153·2
149·4	146·9	139·2	145·0	151·3	151·7	160·9	153·9	166·3	165·4	158·5	157·8	149·7
158·9	149·4	146·4	150·0	156·2	164·8	168·1	160·8	167·5	166·7	159·0	161·8	156·7
157·7	150·8	147·9	157·3	163·8	164·2	177·4	165·7	181·9	181·6	170·1	170·8	167·5

TABLE IX

INDEX OF AVERAGE WEEKLY EARNINGS BY INDUSTRIES
MEN
AVERAGE 1948 = 100

SIC Order	I	II	III	IV	V	VI			VII	VIII	IX
	Agriculture, Forestry and Fishing	Mining and Quarrying	Treatment of Non-Metalliferous Mining Products	Chemical and Allied Trades	Metal Manufacture	Total Shipbuilding, Engineering and Electrical Goods	Shipbuilding	Engineering	Vehicles	Metal Goods N.E.S.	Precision Instruments, Jewellery, etc.
Annual ([1])											
1949	104·4	103·8	105·1	104·8	103·0	102·7	97·2	103·8	101·6	103·7	104·6
1950	107·2	108·3	110·3	110·3	108·0	107·5	100·0	109·1	107·4	110·1	110·4
1951	114·6	121·4	122·9	122·0	117·4	118·2	109·5	120·5	115·0	118·9	119·0
1952	123·4	134·3	131·6	128·8	127·9	130·4	122·5	132·2	124·8	129·4	128·4
1953	131·2	139·1	140·0	139·3	133·2	138·2	129·3	139·5	134·6	136·6	137·2
1954	139·8	147·1	149·5	149·8	144·0	149·1	137·8	151·4	145·1	147·9	146·4
1955	150·2	156·7	162·9	164·5	157·7	163·6	153·1	165·2	159·0	163·0	158·8
1955—April	147·8	156·9	160·5	162·8	155·5	162·2	152·4	163·6	157·7	160·6	155·1
October	152·6	166·6	165·2	166·2	159·9	164·9	153·7	166·7	160·4	165·3	162·4
1956—April	156·7	173·1	172·3	173·8	169·6	176·3	170·3	177·1	167·2	171·7	169·2

([1]) The 'Annual' figures are averages of the figures for April and October.
([2]) The figures of earnings cover Agriculture only.
([3]) Only that part of the order covered by the Ministry of Labour's Earnings Enquiries.

X	XI	XII	XIII	XIV	XV	XVI	XVII			XVIII	XIX	XXII
											(³)	(³)
Total Textiles	Cotton	Leather, Leather Goods and Fur	Clothing	Food, Drink and Tobacco	Manufacture of Wood and Cork	Paper and Printing	Other Manufacturing Industries	Total Building and Contracting	Building	Gas, Water and Electricity	Transport and Communications	Public Administration and Defence
106·2	105·8	104·3	107·0	105·2	105·6	107·2	103·0	104·5	104·5	103·5	102·9	104·2
113·1	110·3	111·0	111·1	108·7	112·1	113·3	109·0	110·3	109·8	108·0	105·4	106·0
125·1	126·0	119·4	117·7	119·0	124·3	123·5	120·9	124·5	123·6	119·4	116·0	116·6
128·2	120·0	123·7	123·7	127·6	131·6	133·4	125·2	133·6	133·0	128·5	125·0	126·5
141·8	133·5	135·7	134·2	134·9	140·3	144·5	136·6	143·0	142·6	134·4	131·2	132·9
150·7	144·4	142·9	138·7	144·8	148·9	153·4	148·2	151·6	150·7	142·6	142·6	139·6
159·4	148·1	154·2	149·7	157·7	159·1	166·4	160·9	166·2	165·4	159·1	158·6	151·1
156·2	146·7	149·4	147·4	154·5	153·1	162·8	157·9	165·6	164·8	158·7	156·5	147·8
162·5	149·4	158·9	152·0	160·8	165·0	170·0	163·8	166·7	166·0	159·4	160·8	154·4
164·4	151·5	157·7	160·7	167·6	164·3	177·7	166·9	181·0	180·7	170·4	169·4	165·8

TABLE X

INDEX OF AVERAGE WEEKLY EARNINGS BY INDUSTRIES
WOMEN
AVERAGE 1948 = 100

SIC Order	I	II	III	IV	V	VI			VII	VIII	IX
	(²)					Total Shipbuilding, Engineering and Electrical Goods					
	Agriculture, Forestry and Fishing	Mining and Quarrying	Treatment of Non-Metalliferous Mining Products	Chemical and Allied Trades	Metal Manufacture	Total Shipbuilding, Engineering and Electrical Goods	Shipbuilding	Engineering	Vehicles	Metal Goods N.E.S.	Precision Instruments, Jewellery, etc.
Annual (¹)											
1949	104·3	110·5	107·3	105·4	103·9	105·9	101·3	106·1	106·0	104·8	106·5
1950	105·2	116·9	110·1	111·1	108·1	110·1	103·0	109·9	111·1	109·2	110·4
1951	113·1	122·6	119·7	121·5	117·0	118·6	110·7	118·9	116·8	117·8	117·8
1952	120·2	135·1	127·7	133·5	128·9	132·5	122·8	132·8	129·1	130·0	127·9
1953	128·4	144·0	133·9	141·6	134·3	142·0	133·6	140·9	139·1	137·2	135·9
1954	132·0	150·4	143·0	146·0	147·7	151·3	139·4	152·1	148·0	146·0	144·3
1955	141·1	161·2	152·7	158·3	158·0	162·9	148·9	163·3	158·4	156·7	155·6
1955—April	138·4	158·6	151·8	156·1	156·9	162·5	147·1	162·8	157·6	155·6	154·2
October	143·8	163·7	153·6	160·4	159·1	163·3	150·7	163·7	159·3	157·7	156·9
1956—April	149·4	170·7	155·7	167·0	167·6	171·4	165·7	173·0	164·0	164·9	161·0

(¹) The 'Annual' figures are averages of the figures for April and October.
(²) The figures of earnings cover Total Females in Agriculture only.
(³) Only that part of the order covered by the Ministry of Labour's Earnings Enquiries.

X		XI	XII	XIII	XIV	XV	XVI	XVII		XVIII	XIX	XXII
											(¹)	(²)
Total Textiles	Cotton	Leather, Leather Goods and Fur	Clothing	Food, Drink and Tobacco	Manufactures of Wood and Cork	Paper and Printing	Other Manufacturing Industries	Total Building and Contracting	Building	Gas, Water and Electricity	Transport and Communications	Public Administration and Defence
106·3	105·0	104·2	107·5	106·2	106·0	102·8	103·5	105·5	112·2	101·8	103·8	111·1
112·6	109·9	108·4	112·0	110·2	112·4	108·4	108·4	106·5	112·3	99·1	105·4	115·4
125·6	125·7	116·8	118·6	119·7	122·6	117·3	117·8	114·8	121·0	109·8	118·0	123·5
126·0	120·6	123·4	122·6	129·4	133·8	133·9	126·2	123·4	130·0	120·6	128·4	135·9
139·6	134·9	132·6	133·9	136·7	140·7	142·6	133·3	128·1	134·8	127·4	133·9	142·2
146·9	145·0	139·7	138·9	143·2	147·2	147·6	141·9	134·0	140·9	133·1	144·6	149·0
153·1	149·0	148·7	148·2	155·1	157·8	155·9	150·2	145·1	153·9	144·5	157·8	158·7
150·4	148·2	145·5	146·0	152·4	149·2	153·6	147·7	142·2	151·5	144·7	157·0	154·2
155·8	149·7	151·8	150·3	157·7	166·3	158·1	152·6	147·9	156·3	144·2	158·7	163·1
157·3	150·6	154·3	1571·	164·1	164·2	169·1	157·7	158·4	168·7	160·3	168·6	174·2

GEORGE ALLEN & UNWIN LTD
London: 40 Museum Street, W.C.1

Auckland: 24 Wyndham Street
Sydney, N.S.W.: Bradbury House, 55 York Street
Cape Town: 109 Long Street
Bombay: 15 Graham Road, Ballard Estate, Bombay 1
Calcutta: 17 Chittaranjan Avenue, Calcutta 13
New Delhi: 13–14 Ajmeri Gate Extension, New Delhi 1
Karachi: Karachi Chambers, McLeod Road
Mexico: Villalongin 32–10, Piso, Mexico 5, D.F.
Toronto: 91 Wellington Street West
São Paulo: Avenida 9 de Julho 1138-Ap. 51
Buenos Aires: Escritorio 454–459, Florida 165
Singapore: 36c Prinsep Street, Singapore 7
Hong Kong: 1/12 Mirador Mansions, Kowloon

NATIONAL INCOME
AND ECONOMIC GROWTH

KENNETH KURIHARA

This new book by Professor Kurihara is intended as a textbook for intermediate students of Macroeconomic Theory. It is rather more advanced and comprehensive than his *Introduction to Keynesian Dynamics* and less specialized and polemical than his *Keynesian Theory of Economic Development*. It includes a number of fresh techniques of analysis.

The book makes a pioneering effort to integrate national income accounting, income-employment theory, and growth analysis into a unified whole. Inclusion of the last-named subject is based on Professor Kurihara's belief that growth economics is taught most effectively as a dynamic implication of basic national income theory. Accordingly, the book contains a much fuller treatment of economic growth than the prevailing national income texts do.

Addressed to the complex and pivotal problem of achieving the highest feasible rate of growth of real national income while maintaining full employment without inflation, the book is expressly confined to the clarification of the technical aspects of the problem. Yet Professor Kurihara endeavours to make allusion to practical application and broad 'determinants of determinants' throughout in the varying context of a modern mixed open economy with its dynamic interaction of the private, the public, and the foreign-trade sectors.

Demy 8vo. About 25s. net

THE NEO-CLASSICAL THEORY
OR ECONOMIC THEORY

J. E. MEADE

Professor Meade has outlined the way in which classical economic analysis may be developed for application to the problem of economic growth. This is a book for the student of economic theory; but the basic theory is expounded in the main text of this book in a way which does not demand any extensive familiarity with mathematical techniques.

Demy 8vo. 25s. net

BREAKAWAY UNIONS
AND THE SMALL TRADE UNION

SHIRLEY W. LERNER

This book examines inter-union disputes and trade union history from an entirely fresh angle. Necessarily it is based on primary sources and it is far from academic in its style and in its interest, since it is able to reveal the human reactions involved in one of the most intractable spheres of industrial relations. Here are the roots of some of the more difficult labour problems of our time.

Dr Lerner has made a number of case studies. The first demonstrates the difficult relationship of the small union with more powerful unions. The second shows that the T.U.C. is inclined to ignore rank-and-file wishes when it seeks to settle jurisdictional disputes and how such disregard of members' feelings brings fresh problems in its train. A third study traces the exciting birth and death of a Communist breakaway union in the London clothing industry, which demoralized and disorganized East End workers between 1928 and 1935, while the fourth analyses the causes of secessions from a civil service union. This study demonstrates the role of the political parties and of government when confronted with inter-union disputes'

Demy 8vo. 25s. net

CASES AND PROBLEMS IN
ECONOMICS

Z. S. DUESENBERRY, L. E. PRESTON

The teachings of economics on the basis of real-life problems is gaining ground, but we are still indebted to America for adequate source material. The two experienced authors have provided 'a large stock of excellent problems . . . culled from real life which will be a great boon to us'—to quote from our adviser's report—'and a very important and welcome contribution to the material available for teaching economics in this country'.

Demy 8vo. 15s. net

INDIAN ECONOMIC
POLICY AND DEVELOPMENT

P. T. BAUER

In this important new book Prof Bauer reviews the major elements of official Indian development policy, considers their economic implications and their probable political and economic results. He then examines alternative approaches to the promotion of development. The development plans, notably the Second Five Year Plan and the official outlines of the Third Plan, receive major attention, but the author also considers other official policies and measures affecting economic development, which do not usually figure prominently in the formal development plans. He reviews the Indian economic and social scene, since without an understanding of this background it is impossible to assess the merits of alternative policies and methods.

Specific themes which Prof Bauer considers are: the influence of social customs and attitudes on economic progress; the relationship between investment expenditure and economic development; inter-relationships between agriculture and industry; the heavy industry programme; the controls over the private sector; the relation of Plan finance to the foreign exchange crisis; the role of foreign aid; and the importance of certain major political objectives.

The author is Professor of Economics (with special reference to under-developed countries and economic development) at the London School of Economics.

Demy 8vo. 16s. net

THE USE OF ECONOMIC STATISTICS

C. A. BLYTH

An elementary introduction to the sources of economic statistics and their uses in answering economic questions.
Minerva Series of Students' Handbooks.

Demy 8vo. 28s. net

THE RULING SERVANTS

E. STRAUSS

This book attacks one of the most important and controversial problems of today—the origins and prospects of bureaucracy. It gives a most lucid analysis of the bureaucratic defects of modern mass organizations and these are illustrated with a wealth of detail. But its main subject is the change in the balance of power between legislators and administrators in government, and between the rank-and-file and the party machines in politics. The author believes that bureaucratic rule results from strong tension between hostile interests interfering with effective outside control over the administration.

This theme is stated in two analytical chapters and then developed in three substantial essays on the political development of Russia, France and Britain. The concluding chapter discusses the chances of improving public control of the administration of government and it ends with a warning of the threat to real political democracy inherent in rigid party machines.

Demy 8vo. 30s. net

THE PRICE OF T.U.C. LEADERSHIP

BRYN ROBERTS

In this work the General Secretary of a large trade union makes serious criticism of the T.U.C. leadership, contending, among other things, that it bears responsibility for Labour's defeat in the 1959 General Election, and for the decline in the influence and effectiveness of the trade union movement.

Prevailing trade union disorder and the frequency of unofficial strikes are also attributed to the failure of the T.U.C. leadership to guide and direct the 8,337,325 members it claims to represent. The author makes other severe criticism of the leadership, describing its public relations and how its elections are conducted.

Demy 8vo. 16s. net

GEORGE ALLEN & UNWIN LTD